THE AIRSHIP VC

THE AIRSHIP VC

The life of Captain William Leefe Robinson

By

Raymond Laurence Rimell

This book is dedicated to the memory of Ernest, Katherine, Grace, Irene, Ruth, Harold and William.

Published in 1989 by Aston Publications Limited
Bourne End House, Harvest Hill
Bourne End, Bucks SL8 5JJ

© Raymond Laurence Rimell 1989

British Library Cataloguing in Publication Data
Rimell, Raymond Laurence
  The Airship VC.
  1. Great Britain. Civil aviation. Robinson, William Leefe
  I. Title
  387.7'092'4

  ISBN 0 946627 53 3

Sole distributors to the UK book trade,
Springfield Books Limited
Norman Road, Denby Dale
Huddersfield, West Yorkshire HD8 8TH

Sole distributors for the USA,
Motorbooks International
Osceola, Wisconsin 54020
United States

Printed in England by Redwood Burn Limited.

ACKNOWLEDGEMENTS

The *Airship VC* is the result of many years' research, during which time the first fully documented version of the William Leefe Robinson story appeared as a chapter in one of the author's previous works, *Zeppelin!* Of necessity it was a much abbreviated account and now, with this full-length biography, a great deal of additional material can be incorporated, much of it for the first time since the end of 'The Great War'. The complete story could not have been told, however, without the full co-operation and enthusiasm freely extended to the author by Captain Robinson's nieces, Mrs R. G. (Gia) Libin and Mrs Rose David, to whom he owes a great debt of gratitude. Their willingness to share their precious family archives and memories with the author was a rare privilege and has done a great deal to 'round out' the portrait of their late uncle which is presented in these pages.

Also to those who supplied many fascinating anecdotes, private correspondence and cherished photographs, I am deeply grateful: Miss Mary Sowrey; Air Marshal Sir Frederick B. Sowrey, KCB, CBE, AFC, and Captain S. R. Stammers' sister, Mrs Vera Tate. Thanks are also due to the following for their long-term assistance and encouragement: Mr Peter Amesbury; Mr J. R. Barfoot; Mr M. Clark; Major E. N. Clifton; Mr Peter Cooksley; Mr J. Colinson; Mr Barrington Gray; Mr W. A. Fox, Bursar of St Bees; Mr K. E. Hagen; Mrs C. Hervey; Squadron Leader H. E. Hervey; Mr Erik Hildesheim; Messrs C. and P. Kirby; Mr G. W. Lees, Headmaster (Ret.) of St Bees; Mr G. S. Leslie; Mr R. W. Raby of the Civic Centre, Harrow; Group Captain W. S. O. Randle, CBE, AFC, DFM; Mr Colin Rust of Stanmore for untiring assistance with Captain Robinson's Harrow Weald connections; Mrs K. Rimell; Mr K. Thomas, BSc; Mr R. Warner; Mr D. Whetton and the staff of the British Newspaper Library; the Cater Museum; the Essex Records Office; the General Register Office of the Harrow Civic Centre; the Hertsmere UDC; the Imperial War Museum; the Ministry of Defence; Pinner Library; the POW 1914/18 Dining Club; the Public Records Office; the Royal Air Force Museum and the Regimental HQ of the Worcestershire and Sherwood Foresters Regiment. Thanks should also be accorded to the editors of local newspapers and periodicals in Essex, Hertfordshire, London and Middlesex who latterly published the author's appeals for wartime eyewitnesses and to the many people of those areas who responded as a result.

The author is also indebted to various publishers for permission to use extracts and illustrations from the following: *The Barnet Press*; *The Daily Express*; *The Daily Mail*; *The Daily Mirror*; the Essex Records Office; *The Harrow Observer*; the Imperial War Museum; the Public Records Office; the RAF Museum and *The Times*.

Finally the author wishes to thank Mr and Mrs L. W. W. Rimell and Mrs A. Hogan for their continual support and encouragement; Mr J. M. Bruce, ISO, MA, FrHistS, FRAeS, and Dr D. H. Robinson for research assistance with British and German aerial operations respectively; Richard Bishop, associate director, Coins and Medals department of Christie's, James Hammond and press officer Peter Rose, alsoof Christie's; Mrs Julie Stilwell for originally transcribing all of Captain Robinson's surviving letters and, last but by no means least, Mrs Fiona Parker who typed the completed manuscript.

Despite the assistance rendered by so many, it in no way relieves the author of his responsibility in presenting an accurate version of the events as portrayed in this book. Any errors, either of fact or omission, are entirely of his own making.

R. L. Rimell

CONTENTS

Appendices

FOREWORD

By Mrs R. G. Libin, niece of Captain W. L. Robinson, VC.

Surely most readers will wish to skip reading a Foreword and turn straight to the main subject of this book, the life of my uncle, William Leefe Robinson. Yet it is because of him that the author walked into my life and made it clear that among my family memorabilia he was seeking material for his first book, *Zeppelin!* At a time when some of us erroneously regarded many young people as devoid of purpose and personal drive, Raymond Rimell struck me at once as someone prepared to take painstaking trouble to gather facts for a book that resulted in most interesting reading. This was followed by the accomplishment of the present volume, all the more remarkable because he had the imagination to place himself into the historic times of Uncle Billy's life. This imagination, I was told, being fired when Raymond, as a young boy, passed the Leefe Robinson restaurant near Uncle Billy's grave. The sad thing for Education is that his ability was unrecognized during his educational years.

My mother Kitty was the eldest sister who, as a vivid story-teller, used to recount to me endless stories about her baby brother Billy. To me, Uncle Billy was dashing, handsome and full of fun, but above all he had a tender heart for all living things that suffered. During my years as a school teacher, I reasoned that since Billy had not lived to have his own children, he would have wished me to help sick children, to give them hope and something to look forward to, such as a holiday after their cancer treatment. I feel certain that by auctioning his VC and creating the charity 'A Medal For Life' for this purpose, Billy would regard his spirit as active and alive. This, then, is the heritage he left us.

Gia Libin, Chairman, A Medal for Life.

PREFACE

The Christmas of 1918 had come and gone. For most people the seasonal festivities were doubly joyous, for November had seen the end of the bitterest, bloodiest war ever. During the years of World War I, over 13,000,000 fighting men went to their deaths on land, sea and in the air; there was hardly a single family in the entire civilized world left untouched by personal grief and tragedy. As if the wartime casualties were not terrifying enough, the globe was now in the midst of a deadly influenza pandemic; millions contracted it and millions died. At Harrow Weald, Middlesex, on 3 January, 1919, they buried another victim of the virus, just one among many. But this was no ordinary funeral, for hundreds of people had turned up on this first Friday of the new year.

During the morning the crowds had been growing until forward progress on the roads leading from Stanmore and Wealdstone was virtually impossible so heavy were the numbers. They climbed fences and trees for vantage points, they jostled and shoved for prime positions, the narrow lane passing Brockhurst Corner and All Saints Church was a virtual mass of humanity. They came from all walks of life: the poor, the rich, the civilian, the serviceman, the member of parliament, the local dignitary, the churchman, the close friends and relatives and policemen – policemen everywhere. Specially-printed memorial cards were exchanging hands rapidly as the hour of interment grew closer, the crowd were expectant and mostly silent. There was a subdued hubbub of conversation, then the sound of horses' hooves between the squeak of carriage wheels and, somewhere in the background, a dull droning which grew into a deep throaty roar, heralding a flight of six biplanes from the Royal Air Force, the resonant clatter of their engines all but drowning the muffled peal of bells from the church tower as they swept overhead.

Along with scores of others, schoolboy George Collinson watched spellbound as one of the fighters left the formation and, its motor throttled back, began to circle around a nearby house. A gasp went up from several quarters as a dark object fell from the aeroplane to land in the grounds of Lavender Cottage; the mystery object bounced once and lay still. Someone came out of the cottage, picked up the large circle of laurels and disappeared inside. He placed the wreath upon a flag-draped coffin that had been standing in the hallway for some time, a coffin that contained the body of a 23-year-old flying officer who had died four days previously.

As the moving strains of Beethoven's funeral march wafted over the now-hushed audience, George Collinson opened up his silver and black-bordered memorial card and scanned the contents. The brief inscription recorded that Captain Leefe Robinson, VC, the 'first Airman who brought down a Zeppelin at Cuffley in Sept. 1916' had died on Tuesday, 31 December, 1918. There was also an anonymous piece of verse alongside a fuzzy portrait of a handsome young man in Royal Flying Corps uniform:

'Now the labourer's task is o'er,
Now the battle-day is past;
Now, upon the farther shore,
Stands the voyager at last;
Father, in Thy gracious keeping,
Leave me now Thy servant sleeping,
Life's work well done,
Life's race well run,
Life's crown well won,
    Now comes rest.'

So passed William Leefe Robinson, one of World War I's most popular heroes. His name may not be found among the long lists of wartime Allied air aces, but his name today is as well remembered as those of Ball, McCudden, Guynemer and Richthofen. For Robinson's award-winning achievement was played out in front of an audience of thousands and led the way to the eventual defeat of Germany's airship bombers.

R. L. Rimell, Berkhamsted, September 1989

CHAPTER ONE

ORIGINS

Sunday, 11 August, 1907
Bishop Cotton School

My darling Irene and Ruth,

I am so sorry I have not written to answer your nice birthday letters before now, but I have had so many letters to write and only Sunday to write them on. It was so good of you both to have written. I do so like to have every little detail about Coorg; I often think of the jolly times we had together. I and Harold are in the first form, I find the lessons a little hard, but Harold can do them alright and is third to the top of the form.

Both of us are in the Cadet Corps and we go to parade every Saturday. I find it is not all play by any means.

Your loving brother,
Willie.

William Braham Robinson was born in June 1819, the only son of Lieutenant Abraham Robinson RN, who boasted a family line of distinctly nautical connections stretching back well into the 18th century. In July 1835 Abraham arranged for his young son to embark on a seven-year shipbuilding apprenticeship after which Braham was made draughtsman for a salary of six shillings a day. His career in the industry was a highly successful one and in 1869 he was appointed Master Shipwright and Engineer of HM Dockyard Portsmouth, the title later changed to Chief Constructor, and served with distinction in this capacity until his retirement in 1881.

Braham had married Caroline Portch Sturgess at Gillingham in 1845 and she would eventually bear him five sons and three daughters. By all accounts Braham was a proud and devoted father, devastated at the short illness and death of his five-year-old son Ernest at Sheerness. Three other sons, Francis, Mark and Horace, were all in their turn sent away to school at Cranbrook, Kent, where the boys found boarding at the old Elizabethan building a lot less comfortable than living at home. When Braham was appointed master shipwright and sent to Malta in 1862, Francis was already serving with the fleet as a midshipman and to the other brothers' delight their parents took the family with them across France. There was no school for them in Malta, but they sailed across the harbour every day to their tutor. The family were to stay in Malta for over two years.

Horace, born on 10 November, 1851, grew into a tall, handsome and charming man of great compassion and, like his father, a keen liberal, forming a particularly strong regard for Gladstone. During his early twenties Horace was introduced to young Elizabeth Eshe Leefe by some of her cousins from Yorkshire, where her father, David Leefe, had been a farmer-owner. Horace was quickly smitten and offered Elizabeth his hand in marriage, but she turned him down mainly, it is believed, because of her suitor's fanatical devotion to the cause of teetotalism, a cause vigorously championed by his father. William and Caroline had 'signed the pledge' on their wedding day, Braham having been appalled by the widespread drunkenness of sailors in the Royal Navy.

Young Horace boasted a fine baritone voice and enjoyed singing at the frequent Saturday night amateur concerts held during winter months at a hall near the Portsmouth dockyards. The entertainments were usually organized by his father and, unsurprisingly, often included talks by well-known personalities on the subject of temperance. In 1879 Horace married Alice Holding, but tragically she died the following year. Not long after, Horace renewed his acquaintance with Elizabeth Leefe and finally won her over, proposed once again and this time was accepted.

In 1883, Elizabeth's widowed mother was living at Penge, near the Crystal Palace, and it was there on 19 September that the young couple's first child was born, a boy, named Ernest in memory of Horace's tragic younger brother.[1] Shortly afterwards the Robinsons sailed for India to make their home at Pollibetta, South Coorg, near Mercara, where Horace was to own and manage the Kaima Betta coffee estate, bought for him by his father.

The life of a coffee planter during the late 1880s was by no means an easy one and many Europeans made and lost their fortunes within the turn of a season. Coffee was the most difficult of crops to cultivate. It required a climate free from extremes of heat and moisture − if too dry the plants would not blossom freely; after really wet seasons they fell easy prey to pests and diseases. There were valleys in southern India about that time into which planters had invested tens of thousands of pounds and from which only a handful of good crops had been picked. When Horace and Bessie, as his wife was affectionately known to her family and friends, arrived in India the prospects for the coffee industry were brighter following several good seasons. The family lived in a large bungalow at Kaima Betta and in the years that followed Bessie bore a further six children: Katherine, Grace, Irene, Ruth and Harold, who was born in England at the family's house, Tennyson Villa, in Boscombe, 'a short walk from the sea', and near to the children's guardian, Lady Alabaster. The youngest was William, who drew his first breath at Kaima Betta on 14 July, 1895. All the children were given Elizabeth's maiden name of Leefe as their second Christian name, but rarely, if ever, referred to it other than by initial.

In 1901 the fortunes of the coffee industry in India were reversed following Brazil's entry into the export market and so the Robinsons temporarily returned to England, first staying at Boscombe then moving to Oxford, where Harold and William began their education by enrolling as day boys with The Dragon School. By 1903 the family was back in India once more, where the inseparable brothers resumed their studies at the Bishop Cotton School in Bangalore:

'Billy was always the favourite as he was always full of mischief, which delighted us. He was always up to jokes and at lessons asking our governess the most awkward questions, especially scripture! He and his brother Harold were up to pranks in every way. We four girls found it most amusing but our governess threatened to leave so the family of Robinsons had to go!'[2]

In India William enjoyed all the advantages that come to the seventh-born of a close-knit family unit. Doubtless somewhat indulged by his parents and pampered by four adoring older sisters, young Billy's early years were full of mischievous fun with schooling somewhat low down on his list of priorities.

Horace and Elizabeth's eldest daughters, Katherine, Grace and Irene, once their education was completed, became tutors to the many English planters' families in the surrounding districts. In 1908 Irene, by then an attractive dark-haired 19-year-old, was teaching in Mangalore and kept in regular touch with her family. Writing from Bishop Cotton School on 12 July, Harold responded to one of his sister's previous letters:

'. . . I am third in my form out of six boys, which is something of a beginning, but I soon mean to become top. We don't get much rain here, only occasionally, but when it does come, I don't know what to do. I suppose you are getting a good dose of it being near the coast. Time seems to fly, for it does not seem as if I have been at the school a month and it seems as if you went only yesterday. However, time does fly past when you are doing something, though it must seem very tiring and tedious for you teaching. If only father had better prospects, it would not cause you to go and earn your living, as well as G and Kit, as you do.

'I daresay I am talking in a very "high" or uppish way, yet still I cannot help thinking of them, and I often long for the time when money is less scarce . . .'[3]

Towards the end of 1909 both William and Harold had sailed back for England, where they were to complete their education, and during September they enrolled at St Bees School on the coast of Cumberland, now Cumbria. St Bees was a long-established and well-respected academy which was opened way back in 1586 following a charter granted in 1583 by Queen Elizabeth I to Edmund Grindal, the then Archbishop of Canterbury, to found a grammar school for boys living in Cumberland and Westmorland. Until the middle of the 19th century the majority of pupils were local, but gradually the school accepted boys from all parts of the country. During the 1800s St Bees was greatly expanded with several new buildings, and facilities increased greatly as a result. Expansion was particularly rapid between 1903 and 1916 under the headmastership of Canon Robert Sawyer, in whose final year there were 350 boys from all over the world on the register. Several additional properties in the village were acquired or leased to accommodate the rising number of boarders, but once the war was over, several houses being considered unsuitable, it was decided that the number of pupils should be reduced. During the last two decades there has once again been a major expansion of accommodation and facilities. The school is now fully co-educational and pupils number almost 400.

At St Bees William won friends easily, becoming popular with boys and masters alike. Although the first to admit to his academic shortcomings, he was poor at spelling, William revelled in all forms of sport and in addition to playing hockey and enjoying sculling, became a useful member of the First XV. He also had a good ear for music, boasting a fine singing voice, with a natural talent for playing a variety of instruments, including the banjo, flute and mouth organ.

During the five years the Robinson brothers were at St Bees, they boarded in Eaglesfield House, their housemaster being Mr F. R. Burnett − known to all the boys as 'Soapy'. During the school holidays they usually lived with various families in the area and enjoyed in particular their times with a Mrs Wise in Keswick:

'. . . You will wonder no doubt at our address being Keswick, but Mr Burnett suddenly wrote on Tuesday saying he had written to Mrs Wise telling her we were coming that day, so we quickly packed and went off by the afternoon train.

'We arrived at Keswick station about 4.15, when we took a cab and drove up here. This is quite a large house, a mile out of Keswick with a glorious view of the surrounding country, which consists of velvety green fields and a glittering lake of diamonds, surrounded by lofty wooded mountains, whose snow-tipped summits sparkle in the sunlight . . .

'. . . (I) have a beautifully snug bedroom commanding a lovely view and a nice cosy sitting room in which we have all meals brought.

'Mrs Wise is *so* kind; she has two sons abroad, one in Africa, the other in America. Hayes (a schoolfellow who lives in Keswick) has invited us to a whist drive this evening, to which we are going. Thank you very much for the stamps enclosed in your letter . . .'

Like any young teenage boys, the brothers enjoyed life away from the classroom to the full and William, in particular, had an eye for the girls:

'. . . I suppose Harold has told you all about our Keswick trip. I had a *fine* time taking one of the chap's sisters, Ruby Jenkinson by name, about. She is deuced pretty. Then there was Ethel Waters, Doris Iredale and Dorothy Wise there as well. By jove! Some of the chaps were envious! And one of them snapped me with Ruby . . .'[4]

Both Billy and Harold corresponded frequently with their sisters and parents, relating their scholastic successes and failures in light-hearted vein. In the New Year of 1912 William wrote to his father:

'I am so sorry to hear you have not had a very pleasant Christmas owing to your toothache, but trust that you will have quite recovered by the time this letter reaches you. I remember in a letter of yours you asked me to promise you that I will *never* smoke or drink. I will do so with all my heart and take a pride in keeping a promise I know to be so difficult to accomplish, indeed a promise that is not is a *very* sorry thing.

'Yes – I promise that while I have the use of my hands and fists, and also my mind and tongue I will never contaminate my mouth with accursed liquor or a damned cigarette or anything else connected with them – it is bad language, but then I think it is pardonable in such cases. But I must tell you some news.

'You see we were all back in Workington after a *most delightful* visit to Keswick.

'It snowed quite fast all yesterday, it stopped late last night and is fine today, although it is a little cold and cloudy.

'I like the snow awfully and hope to have all kinds of fun at St Bees what with snowballing, sledging and skating.

'I hope we go to Keswick next holidays; they say it is lovely at Easter and Mrs Wise and family are so good and kind to us. Poor old Mrs Green is also *very, very* kind to us, but everybody seems to be the same, but Workington *is* an old hole . . .'[5]

The summer holidays for 1912 were already being planned in January by the Robinsons and the boys were expecting to spend the break in France – instead they were destined for Kurland in Russia to stay at Berghof, an imposing mansion owned by Baroness von der Recke. The Robinson and Recke families had first become acquainted in India and as a result the Baroness had asked Katherine to stay with her for a while acting as tutor of English and pianoforte to her family and wide circle of friends. At the Baroness's invitation, Irene joined her sisters at Berghof in June and the two boys arrived during August with Grace following sometime later. The holiday was a resounding success, so much so in fact that it was allowed to extend into the first three weeks of the St Bees' autumn term, much to William's delight:

'My darling Mother,

'Just fancy only one more week for the end of the holidays, it only seems yesterday since we came here; but yet it doesn't, because we have got so used to Russian surroundings and to the Germans and Russians themselves that it seems as if we have spent years out here!

'Well, I will try and tell you about our doings here. Last Sunday morning Kitty, Irene, Harold and I all went, after breakfast, for a beautiful long walk; we went on and on by the riverside, and talked about old times and dear old KB. Oh, mother darling, you *don't know* how lovely it is to see some of your family after so long being separated from them, this trip to Russia could *not* have been a better success; the very fact of travelling in a foreign country is an education which you could obtain in no other way, but the *best* part of it all is being with dear old Rene and Kitty again, it links us together once more and makes us feel that we really have got some sisters.

'Kitty is wonderfully stronger and better or else she could *never* have walked as she did that day. In the evening Harold, Irene and Baroness May went to post and when they had gone some time Kitty and I went to meet them, and had a *glorious* talk together.

'Monday morning saw Kitty leave us for her trip with the Recke girl at Elisenhof.

'The same morning the Bahlen girls were to have come to lunch, but they did not turn up until tea time as they had visitors or something. When they did come, Irene, Harold and I took the younger one off to the little river, while the elder stayed behind to amuse May.

'Yesterday – Tuesday – Irene, Harold and I got up earlier than usual (at 7.30), had breakfast at 8 and all three started out to see how far we could boat up the little river. It was a *perfect* morning with the freshness of a late summer and with a friendly warm sun beating down upon us and set in a sky of cloudless blue; it was a glorious row, prettier scenery could not be imagined. We managed to get as far as we could possibly go which was about 3 miles down, and returned at about 11.30 . . .

'Tons of love to all

Willie.'[6]

Then another letter, this time to his father, a week later:

'You see we are *still* in Russia, you will be surprised no doubt to see the above address as in her last letter mother said she expected we would be on our way home. Don't be alarmed father dear, as we only arrive *two* days late for school if we stay on here a week longer than we thought we could stay.

'I have perhaps expressed myself rather badly giving you the impression that we are staying here *another* week; but I only meant to say that if we start today (as we are doing) we arrive at St Bees on the Sunday instead of the Friday, where as if we had started *last* week, we would have arrived about five days too soon!

'Father dear, you cannot *imagine* what a blessing and a huge success this half has been, and I thank you *most* sincerely for your kind generosity in sending the means to accomplish this lovely holiday . . .'[7]

Irene and Kitty remained in Russia for a time while the boys kept up a steady stream of correspondence to Kurland and South Coorg from Eaglesfield House. On 25 September Harold wrote to Irene:

'As I have a little more time I must really write you something and tell you a little of our travels. It was all right going down to Riga, except when Baroness Recke left us to talk to Princess Lievin and a man at Milan tried to force himself onto Madame's seat. *"Gibber-gibber frei?"* he said, meaning I suppose, "are these seats free?" Billy however thought he was talking French, mistaking *frei* for *frère* for he greatly astonished the poor man by fiercely asserting in English that he wasn't his brother, nor ever likely to be, and that he wouldn't be imposed upon and be called the long-lost relative of anybody. The student was so astounded that he backed out hurriedly murmuring something or other, which if translated must have been to the effect that it was a rash job to carry lunatics on Russian trains.

'It was a ripping surprise seeing Kitty again especially as we thought we would miss her. Baroness Recke was so awfully ripping to us, giving us all sorts of things and seeing us off on the boat. She is a dear and I do love her. There were six passengers in all, counting ourselves, two old men (commoners) and two young girls, about 14 or 17. The latter was very reticent, but Billy as usual started sending out feelers in her direction and wormed his way into talking to her. I knew they were *rather* pally but I discovered afterwards that while I read in the cabin in the afternoon they used to hold clandestine meetings on the deck and I believe Billy actually gained her handkerchief and address before he left. He also took about 24 photos out of 25 of her in that Jicko camera. She rejoices in the name of Muriel Hogg. There's something too piggish about it to please me. Catch Billy for taking every opportunity . . .'[8]

On their return to Cumberland both William and Harold found that their extended break had set them back in their studies, William in particular finding his end-of-term results somewhat discouraging. But there were many distractions to soften his disappointment: trips to the theatre, boating, picnics, an ever-growing circle of young girls and, of course, the rugby matches:

'. . . Last Saturday we all went to Whitehaven to see a County match, Cumberland v Cheshire. There were crowds of people there, over 2000, and the school were allowed to go if they walked there, a distance of 4 miles and back, and they had to be in for tea at school. Of course Bill and I made the excuse that we had to get presents for father or else for someone else (the number of times a boy's pater has birthdays a term whenever they want to go into town, it's ridiculous for they must age most awfully quickly; according to some they must be at least 100 years old) and so of course got leave to stay for tea and train back in time for prep. The match was awfully exciting while Cumberland won by 12 points to 3. The enthusiasm was tremendous, people coming from miles around to see it . . .

'We had an A1 tea at a place called Anderson's, where all the waitresses were under age and some quite pretty!!

'. . . Well, about our Saturday fling. After tea, of which I am certain I was cheated out of at least a shilling (for I didn't bother to look at the change!) we strolled about the streets until six and then made for the station. The train was packed when we got there, of people returning after the match, and so we three (we form a trio on our expeditions with another fellow who's quite as keen as a rag as we are) bought papers and made for an empty 'first' and settled ourselves low in the seats with our papers up. It's a pretty risky job travelling 'first' from Whitehaven, for the porters are pretty smart there. The time before, Bill and this other chap got into one and a porter discovered them curled up. They at first pretended to be asleep, but as they wouldn't act, they had to get out, murmuring "Dear me! fancy mistaking this for a third, very silly of us indeed!" "Of course it ought to have been a third!", etc. That time, however, we got through alright and arrived at St Bees in fine style. I didn't attempt to get under the seat *this* time, thank you, I wasn't going to risk being taken for a man "half a degree over" again . . .'[9]

By the end of the year both Kitty and Grace, the latter by then in nursing service, were back in England joining William and Harold at their uncle's Geraldine Lodge in East Hill, Wandsworth, for the Christmas holidays. Dr Mark Robinson ran his medical practice from the large house, and although there were plenty of rooms, so many members of the family were staying there that Christmas the young Robinson boys had to be put up by Mr and Mrs Davidson in nearby Knoll Road:

'My darling Father,

'On Saturday afternoon, Harold and I went to see G, the house she is at is beastly small and in a horrid part of London and the old man she is nursing is a loathsome old fig, but I believe his old wife is quite decent, but I daresay you have heard all about this from Kitty and G.

'Well, we all went out, and G treated us to a cinema show. G is a perfect dear. She is so generous with her scanty purse, I believe she would spend all she has if we would only let her; when we first came here she gave us half a crown each and fitted us out with hair and nail brushes etc., (things that we had forgotten or lost). And she has given us besides, each a tie, Harold a muffler, and me a pair of socks, and she has treated us to any amount of teas and cinema shows.

'Nothing particular happened on Sunday, except that we went over to Geraldine Lodge in the evening and had a cup of coffee after supper.

'Monday was a very eventful day, as we all went off on a spree to Bournemouth – of course, we could not take G with us, as she was on duty. It was a glorious day, just like early spring, everything looked so gay and happy.

'After a long but lovely train journey we arrived at Bournemouth at about 2 o'clock – having started at 11.38 – when we took a tram to Boscombe Arcade. It was delightful trying to remember all the old places. I was surprised that I remembered as much as I did considering I was about 4 or 5 years old when I left. I remembered the old Arcade I think best of all although it was changed a bit.

'It was awfully funny how small everything seemed. I remember I used to think the Bournemouth streets were huge and the Arcade miles long! Now everything seems to have shrunk, even the houses.

'Well, I must get on to what we did. After looking round a bit we all journeyed down to the Alabasters; they were awfully kind, receiving us with open arms. There we were introduced to three *charming* girls, two Americans and one Swede (I think she was). After coffee and cakes we all went to the rink where I monopolized the prettiest American girl all afternoon. It was g-l-o-r-i-o-u-s. We had tea there and after skating a bit we went to the Alabasters . . .

'Tuesday evening we were given tickets for *The Miracle* at the Covent Garden theatre – it was only in animated pictures but still it was beautiful, the orchestra, singing and general getting up, the whole thing was magnificent; they burnt incense the whole time which had a very realistic effect.

'Wednesday morning we went to the city and went over Westminster Abbey. It is a grand old building, the tombs and monuments especially are fine. Thursday morning we went with Kitty to the Tate Gallery – it was ripping. It is so nice to go round a picture gallery with somebody who understands the pictures – it is quite an education too.

'The general public stride round a building like that glancing at the pictures, regarding them as pieces of canvas with daubs of paint stuck here and there to produce a certain pretty effect. They see no real meaning in these works of art.

'In the afternoon Uncle Mark called for us, and took us home again. It is awfully interesting going about London with him, because he explains all about the buildings, streets, etc.; amongst other things he took us over a part of Guildhall.

'In the evening Harold and I went to the skating rink. When I first went on these holidays I found I had forgotten an awful lot, but I am getting it all back now, and improving − you *don't know* how glorious it is especially when you have someone nice to take round. Oh it's all right, father dear, I'm very careful who I take round.

'This afternoon Kitty, Harold and I are going off with G somewhere or other and this evening dear old Mr Davidson has got us a "box" for *Princess Caprice* at the Shaftesbury.

'Love to all,

'Ever your loving son,

Willie.'[10]

By January 1913 18-year-old William Leefe Robinson seemed to have developed a very clear picture of what the future should hold for him. On the 23rd of the month he wrote to his mother outlining a French holiday with Kitty, his desire to leave St Bees in favour of personal tutelage and, after completing his education, his intention to join the armed services:

'. . . Back at St Bees again. Jove, the climate up here is a bit different from what we had down south. It's all I can do to get warm, it snowed a good bit yesterday, but thank goodness it's all gone by now. I don't mind hard frost if we have skating, but snow I detest, it is nearly always beastly slushy, and very seldom any use for sleighing − at least not in England.

'I saw the book of all the boys' places in the terms and exams marks for the first year yesterday, and I saw how beastly I was, but you mustn't blame me too much for both Harold and I were about 3 weeks absent − every absent day counted − from the term's work and that of course brought our places for the French order and Science order very low. I was absent more times than Harold.

'This is, mother dear, my rough plan for the future. These holidays spend at Bournemouth. It wouldn't be *very* much more expensive would it?

'Next holidays − summer − to be spent with Kitty in *France*, swotting French. I *do* hope this can be arranged (?) Then nothing until *about* April 1914 when I *ought* to leave school and have a private coach − I may share one with some other fellow, so as to reduce expenses − for about six months, on and off, with a few holidays now and then.

'If I am given this chance, I somehow − although I know nothing now − feel *sure* I will pass into the REs; if I do, well and good, if not I think the best plan for me to do is to try again (if I only *just* failed, or if I passed badly in maths) to try Sandhurst and get, if I can, into the Indian army. Then, if I don't find the Indian climate agrees with me, I could either get into the English army, or, if luck smiled upon me, and I made a few influential friends I would go − or have a good try to go − into the *Egyptian* army. It is aiming high I know, but then it is better to aim at the bull than the outer circle: I may at least get an inner . . .'[11]

William's letter breathed with genuine enthusiasm; with the confidence of youthful innocence he had mapped out his destiny but the world, meanwhile, had other plans . . .

CHAPTER TWO

FOR KING AND COUNTRY

A STATE OF WAR

His Majesty's Government informed the German Government on August 4th, 1914, that unless a satisfactory reply to the request of his Majesty's Government for an assurance that Germany would respect the neutrality of Belgium was received by midnight of that day, his Majesty's Government would feel bound to take all steps in their power to uphold that neutrality, and the observance of a treaty to which Germany was as much a party as Great Britain.

The result of this communication having been that his Majesty's Ambassador at Berlin had to ask for his passports, his Majesty's Government have accordingly notified the German Government that a state of war exists between the two countries as from 11 pm today.

British Declaration of War, August 1914

The last year of peace before the world tore itself apart by bloody conflict was a year of change for Horace and Bessie Robinson's sons and daughters as they made their respective plans for futures that never came. Grace married one of her cousins, Arthur Limnell Robinson, son of Horace's brother Mark; the couple subsequently sailing to West Africa, where Arthur found employment as a mining engineer. By early April Irene made her farewells to Kitty and left Russia for England, where she spent the Easter holidays staying at Little Braithwaite Farm to the delight of her younger brothers. By autumn she had returned to India, as had Harold who, having completed his education, was to manage a tea estate. Ruth, who had remained in India, married John W. Irwin in October; they honeymooned in England and the newly-weds stayed there for many months before finally returning to their Jumboor coffee estate in North Coorg. By that time, war clouds were already gathering over Europe.

As for William, he applied himself to his self-appointed task to enter the army and was successful. His final year at St Bees was probably his best. He succeeded his brother as head of Eaglesfield House, was appointed a school prefect and as a sergeant in the OTC had his first taste of military life in manoeuvres held at Mytchett in Kent. Before long his service career would begin in earnest.

History records that the catalyst which sparked World War I was a young Serbian student of Austrian nationality, Gavrilo Princip. On Sunday, 28 June, 1914, at Sarajevo, capital of the Austrian province of Bosnia, Princip pumped three bullets at close range into Archduke Franz Ferdinand and his wife Sophie as they were driven through the streets on an official visit. Within 15 minutes the heirs to the Austro-Hungarian empire were dead. From these shots were sparked the chain of events that spread across Europe and the world in a conflict so far-reaching, so cataclysmic, that humanity would remember it forever as 'The Great War'.

On 4 August crowds milled round the House of Commons and there was a strong feeling of expectancy. Then came the news: it was official, the Declaration of War was issued and cheers rent the air. War fever gripped England with a vengeance; recruiting offices were besieged as thousands of young men offered their services, hoping against hope that they would not be too late and miss all the fighting. Others viewed the situation more soberly; the Foreign Secretary, Sir Edward Grey, managed to find the words that expressed his premonition of impending catastrophe. On the evening of the day war came he was gazing out of his Foreign Office window in Whitehall at a lamplighter working in St James's Park. He turned sadly to a colleague: 'The lamps are going out all over Europe, we shall not see them lit again in our lifetime.'

Ten days later William Leefe Robinson entered the Royal Military College at Sandhurst. As at St Bees, Robinson struck up friendships easily and became hugely popular with his fellow cadets mainly due to his high spirits and irrepressible sense of humour. C. S. Cay remembered him fondly:

'He was one of those happy mortals able to shine at work or play without apparent effort. With all he was extremely modest and I never knew him to lose his temper.'[1]

Robinson was to spend five months at the RMC and by all accounts enjoyed it immensely. A frequent part of the college curriculum was Tactical Exercises Without Troops and the cadets performed these exercises on bicycles. In company with Cadet Cay, Robinson brought up the rear of the troop on one occasion, and passing a village pub noticed a number of dragoons' horses tethered outside. It was hot, and the bike saddles were hard; why not swap their uncomfortable mounts for the four-legged variety? Robinson let down one of his tyres and persuaded Cay to do likewise. Dumping their bikes behind a hedge they quietly led two horses down the road and galloped off to reconnoitre the 'enemy positions' in style. After an exhilarating couple of hours over the Kent countryside they reined in at the pub to be confronted by a pair of 'rather irate dragoons vowing vengeance'.[2]

Several hours later both Cay and Robinson were hauled up in front of their company commander. An explanation was demanded. Robinson answered with the military slogan that had been drummed into him ever since he arrived at Sandhurst: 'Time spent on reconnaissance is seldom wasted', and while the CO seemed placated he wasn't going to let these high-spirited youngsters off so easily. He wondered how it was that both cadets' bicycles suffered punctures simultaneously. William's story that since Cay always followed in his footsteps, he must have run over the same nail, failed to impress their superior. As it was the cadets got off rather lightly with a few extra fatigues.

Cay recalled another occasion:

'There was a most obnoxious bombast in our company, disliked by all. At drill each day, places were changed in the platoon and when it was the turn of the disliked chap to be on the right of the line, and to step smartly forward on the command "Fix bayonets!" and to perform the operation for the others to take their timing from, lo and behold, he couldn't get it out of its scabbard; it was well and truly stuck! Subdued guffaws from all, and our shamefaced comrade had to be replaced. We all guessed who had perpetrated this little comedy with some Seccotine or other form of adhesive.'

Towards the end of 1914, Robinson applied for his commission, hoping that Cay would join the same unit:

'One failing was (that) he couldn't spell, and although my home was in the south, he persuaded me to apply for his county regiment: the Borders. However, as he spelt it "Boarder", to his disgust, as well as mine, he was posted elsewhere!'[3]

'Elsewhere' was the Worcester Regiment and on 16 December, William found himself posted to the Fifth Militia Battalion. When war broke out both Fifth and Sixth 'Special Reserve' battalions had been mobilized at Worcester and thence to their allotted war stations in the Plymouth garrison area. The Fifth was based at Fort Tregantle near Antony in Cornwall, the Sixth at Raglan Barracks, and at these two bases half-trained 'Special Reservists' completed their preparations for the battles on the Western Front. The two battalions, commanded respectively by Lieutenant W. S. Brindle and Lieutenant Colonel F. D. W. Lea Smith, developed into specialized training organizations, sending draft after draft abroad and receiving instead, 'more recruits of every kind'. It appears that Robinson's duties centred on overseeing the intake of new men and as such he saw little chance of joining the men at the Front. The inaction irked him as time dragged on and he yearned for overseas service, putting in several applications for transfer to other units. When off duty the boredom was relieved by visits to Bournemouth and Plymouth as well as theatre-going and afternoon teas with Ruth and John, who by early 1915 had returned from India and were living with the latter's sister at Seaton.[4] William also kept up regular correspondence with Kaima Betta:

'My darling Mother,

'A letter from both you and dear old K. Bites this mail. First of all let's settle money matters. Dear old mother, I wish you *could* get father to give me just a small allowance; it would be such a help, even if it was only a pound or two a month. Mother, you can realize better than the dear old pater how money goes. One *must* go into Plymouth now and again, or else one would die of boredom here – and if you didn't go in with the other fellow, you would be conspicuous – I think you can understand what I mean.

Then of course there is the mess bill, the share of the guests' expenses, subscriptions and so on, which at the end of a month you find you have very little money to spare.

'... By the way Jack had to pay another bill of eleven odd pounds to the RM College the other day. I explained all to him and he told me to explain to father. It is quite alright, I saw the bill; it was for the second set of uniforms, etc., that I had *at* the college – Jack at first thought I had got the stuff *after* leaving the college – but of course, this is not so, as I explained to him. Father may grumble at the A and N stores account but assure him mother dear, that *all* the things were *absolutely* necessary – warm underclothes, and new night suits, etc. (These night suits are the first I have bought since I have been in England – Harold and I used to wear our old Indian ones at school, then I took on H's). Another thing I *must* get at the stores is a decent pair of warm gloves, the ones I bought myself are not good enough.

'So you would advise me to stay in an English regiment, mother? Of course the climate is all in favour of it – and I mean to marry in another seven years, and then again comes the bother of the Indian climate. It's funny, I often wonder what kind of girl I will at last pick up. If she is half, no an eighth, as sweet and good as my dear old mater, I will consider myself the luckiest of men.

'Last Saturday Ruth wired to me to meet them at the Theatre Royal at 2.30 pm. Like a fool I read it "Hotel" Royal and waited there over an hour for them – I afterwards met them at a restaurant – about 5 o'clock, and it appears they had bought a ticket for me for *Drake*, which was on at the theatre – it was stupid of me to have missed them after having left them, however, I met a lot of my regimental friends and we all went to the late show of *Drake* together – and we had quite a jolly time. Yes, I did see something of Kitty O'Faherty – she didn't think it *comme il faut*[5] to be with so many men, however, so she didn't stay long.

'My writing *is* bad, but what can you expect when I'm trying to write in large armchairs and before a fire which makes one want to drop off to sleep at any moment. I haven't heard anything about that African job yet; I'm afraid it's a washout as I'm too young.

'Thursday 9.30 pm (March 4, 1915)

'... we had rather fun this afternoon. Our senior major had all the Hippodrome people down for the afternoon, and they gave us a top hole entertainment. We had it in our new YMCA hut which has been built just outside the Fort. We entertained them all afterwards – about eight girls and four men, it was great sport – we all managed to get into our little officers' mess somehow. I sent Mr Taylor your letter mother, and he was awfully pleased about it. I may go up to town for the weekend if I can get permission, as Mr Taylor is going to his house in Henley on the 13th of the month.

'I'm going to shut up now, best and dearest of mothers, and am going to take to my couch early.

'Aye yr loving son
    Billy.'[6]

Young 'Billy' wrote to his mother again eleven days later, outlining his various duties at the fort:

'. . . I am orderly officer today so I am off duty till twelve midnight. At 10 pm is the sergeant's absentee parade, 10.15 lights out and at 11.15 I have to set out and turn out all the guards and see they are all awake and about their duty. One guard is posted about a mile from the Fort, then when you do come in about 12 o'clock, you generally find some light in a barrack room where men are gambling – I had to "run in" a whole lot of men last time I was orderly officer for gambling at about 12.30. I told you about the drunken captain in command of our company didn't I? Well, he's sent in his papers thank goodness and I have got his job of superintending the digging of fresh trenches between the two Forts, Tregantle and Scabsdon.

'The latest news is that I have sent in my name for the West African job. The only drawback is the climate. I'm told subs get £25 a month besides all kinds of allowances, and at any rate the fighting out there is far more lively and sporting than in France – at any rate at the present stagnant period. But although they want officers out in W. Africa I'm afraid I won't get it as I'm too young, one really ought to be over 21 years of age, and a full lieutenant.

'This war *is* sickening, the other day I heard of the death of a great friend of mine at school – Hawkesworth by name. We all called him "nailer", he was one of the best of fellows. And there are several awfully nice Sandhurst men I knew who have met the same fate – yet I'm longing to get out somehow – I want to be *doing* something.

'Father may wonder at the number of little things I have got at the A and N stores. But I have been quite fair. I have bought things such as brown shoes, socks, buttons and badges, which have cost quite a lot, out of my own money. The watch was an absolute necessity – my old one has been mended so many times and it won't go properly, and a wristwatch is put down as part of our equipment, so I had to get a decent one.

'I told you I was going to spend the afternoon with Jack and Ruth in Plymouth didn't I? Well it was most enjoyable. We had lunch at the Royal Hotel and went to a matinée afterwards – *Business as Usual* review. It was very good and I enjoyed it thoroughly. We had tea at a restaurant and afterwards did a little shopping. Ruth bought an awfully nice dressing case thing for Harold's 21st birthday. I think I will send the old boy my photo and a note just to show I've not forgotten him. Thank the Lord he's not out in France!.

'. . . Last Sunday, five of us subs all had tea at the Whitsand Bay Hotel, an awfully nice hotel about two miles away, I've often had tea – and sometimes dinner – there before now. Yes, I admit with a dear sweet, pretty little girl – now you can't say I hide anything from you, can you? Don't worry my darling mother, you can always be sure your Baby will be steady and will keep his head on his shoulders.'[7]

Robinson's various transfers had been in for some time, but as March wore on he still received no official word and his frustration grew daily. Then towards the end of the month, escape from the sombre Fort Tregantle was afforded by one of his applications finally coming through, a transfer to the Royal Flying Corps. There seems little reason to suppose that Robinson had any great ambition for flying, the subject was never raised in correspondence, more likely the tedium of his position was such that he fired off as many applications as possible and took the first one offered him. Whatever the reasons, on 29 March, 1915, he was posted to No. 4 Squadron RFC based at St Omer in France. William Leefe Robinson was finally going to war.

CHAPTER THREE

BILLY THE BIRDMAN

No. 7 Stationary Hospital,
10 May, 1915

Dear Ruth,

As you can see I am in No. 7 Stationary Hospital, but you are not to worry as I am perfectly alright. We got into a bit of bother over Lille the other day, but my pilot was simply wonderful and had us out of trouble in no time. I'm afraid that I was of no use to him as I was feeling a little Hors de Combat — as you might say — but anyway, all's well that ends well. Tell John I hope to have another drive of the car in the near future and before you go to India, as I shall be coming back to England for more training as soon as I can break out of here. I am going to be a pilot — there's nothing like driving oneself about!

Your ever loving brother,
Billy.

In the early months of 1915 both No. 1 and No. 4 Squadrons, the latter commanded by Major C. A. H. Longcroft, formed the RFC's Third Wing under Lieutenant Colonel H. R. M. Brooke-Popham. By April, No. 4 was mainly equipped with an early version of the Royal Aircraft Factory's BE2c (the initials stood for Blériot Experimental) for reconnaissance and artillery-ranging duties. The BE2c, with its in-built stability, was an ideal platform for such tasks, but this very quality made it vulnerable to manoeuvrable, well-armed German fighters.

Artillery-ranging was not always a particularly easy activity. Robinson and his fellow observers made tracings showing, as accurately as possible, the exact position of each target and the last three artillery salvoes fired thereon as their pilots flew them slowly over the battle area. If the target turned out to be a battery the tracing was to indicate the number of German guns visible and the direction in which they were facing.[1] Early on in the war such information had been transmitted to the ground forces by dropping weighted message bags, but by 1915 the growing use of wireless and aerial photography was providing faster and more reliable results. Judging from the correspondence written during the first weeks of April, young Robinson was clearly enjoying his war:

'My darling old mater,

'I have got about half an hour or so before dinner so I am going to scrawl a few of my thoughts to you just as they come into my head, not caring about the censor or anybody. It is about 6.45 pm and I am sitting in my little room, which is really awfully comfortable.

'I sat down at this desk and took up some of your old letters to me. I hadn't got half through one before I took this sheet of paper, and so here I am writing to the dearest person on earth. I remember in one of your letters you ask if I have a particular hobby, then you remark in rather a wistful way that chasing girls seems to be. What a *very* empty-headed son you must think me my dear old mother, if you really think that of me. Had I the attraction necessary for such a hobby, it is the *last* pastime I would choose. I must mislead you fearfully in my epistles. No, I do have hobbies, but they change about every ten or 12 months according (to how) they interest me. Mathematics took up a good bit of my time during my last school term as you know. I also took up a bit of European history, particularly Spanish – I then read something about telepathy and Sir Oliver Lodge interested me immensely.

'When I passed through London on my way to Plymouth to join my regiment, Kitty took me to the Dore picture gallery and from then onwards I took a very great interest in pictures. I don't know if I have ever told you, but I have often been to the Tate and National galleries.

'. . . of course I have dropped the study since I have been out here. So you see, my dearest old mother, I think about other things besides "Kitty O'Faherties" in my spare hours – girls are alright in their way, but as for making them a hobby?!! Jove! I did laugh at your account of Crystal Palace in your youthful days. What wouldn't I give to be able to look back at those times, and see you in the funny get-up of the time walking demurely in the Crystal Palace gardens under the ever-watchful eye of your mother or old crabby aunt – trying to watch father's glad eyes and encourage them while not giving any yourself. Young and beautiful as you were I daresay it was difficult to keep away from the men's gazes.

'Talking of beauty, you have no idea how beautiful it is above the clouds. I have been up at about 5 o'clock on a still afternoon – you have no idea how glorious it is to gaze at the earth at 7,000 feet or over. But thrilling as that is, the real beauty comes with the clouds. Those rolling wastes of vapour of a hundred shades fading away till they terminate at the horizon into one straight line, or rather circle, which frames your view.'

The same letter, taken up a week later continues:

'I do feel beastly not having written to you all these days – but one never counts time here. It's only by the merest chance that I know this is Sunday and the second of May.

We here very often don't know what month we're in let alone the date and day. Since I left off writing last our squadron has moved about twenty odd miles, we are at another aerodrome now. I love flying more and more every day, and the work is even more interesting than it was.

'There is a small town near the aerodrome and we are billeted there. All our 'Flight' work together, but for sleeping we have separate billets. The people I am with are awfully nice, simply sweet, they gush over you like anything. Compliments are given by the score, and you see me, bowing and scraping, exercising my best French in the vain attempt to show my appreciation of their kindness.

'When I have my early morning doses at 4 and 5 o'clock the old dame and the three *mademoiselles* insist on me taking some coffee before I start in spite of my protestations and declarations that my servant brings me some tea when he wakes me up. One of the girls is really awfully pretty and only about 18 I should say. She's an awfully sweet little thing though rather shy. Well, to go on with the description of this place. Our office is at a farm just near the aerodrome. It's a very decent place but the "farmy" smells which arise sometimes are somewhat overpowering. I spend a good bit of my time at the office being officer i/c photography for the squadron. It is surprising how full of civilians the town is — of course all the wealthy people have left. Those people that do remain have got quite accustomed to the sound of the guns by now. They (the guns) are evidently having a rest today, but they have been very furious. They have often been so frequent that you cannot distinguish one bang from another; it is one continuous rumble. I suppose we have at times had as many as 500 bangs in a minute.

'The papers have just come — and I have just gone out to get the *Sketch* and *Times*. You see we are very well off — we can get practically any paper we like, of course all one day old. It's amusing to read about "our daring air raids", etc., which we know more about than all the papers put together — they do talk bosh sometimes about the RFC too. Yes, it's quite common to hear small boys shouting at the top of their voices with a very funny accent: "Daily Mail, Daily Sketch, Teimes!" It's quaint too to see the English Tommy trying to argue with the boy, perhaps ending up by pulling the youngster's ears, shaking him, and giving him an extra English penny. You would be surprised to see how friendly the Tommies are with all the French people. It is quite a common sight to see Tommies, French girls and women playing with a ball in the street, a kind of street tennis or cricket. They mix up their languages and can talk to one another quite fluently . . .'

William finally concluded his letter the following day:

'My dear, darling old mater, why *will* you worry? I tell you I am as safe here as I ever was or would be with you at KB. The flying corps have had *very, very* few casualties, about 5% I am told . . .

'No, of course I didn't join the corps for the extra pay — although of course it's very nice getting it. I was quite well off in my regiment and am not a penny in debt.

'I get a full observer's pay now, having been made "efficient" about a week ago. Up till then I was getting to 10/6 with allowances; now I get 7/6 (regimented pay) + 5/-

(efficient observer's pay) + allowances (fuel, light and field allowance) which comes to about 4/- or 5/-.

'So you see my total pay per day comes to about 17/-. Of *course* we are *much* better off than the poor trenchites — do they get excellent food and always a lovely comfortable bed with clean sheets? Ye Gods no, I wouldn't swap my position with anyone.

'So good old Harold is in the 99th Deccan Infantry — it sounds "some" regiment doesn't it? Yet I can't imagine Harold looking his best on a horse; still he has plenty of pluck and seems to be getting on beautifully — I'm jolly sure I couldn't jump a hurdle even *with* stirrups now. Fancy Cyril enlisting, it's rather a gamble. I think you *might* get through with some (of) your gentlemanly polish, but you *must* leave some of it behind — and then there is just a chance that you won't get your commission for some years. I wonder why he didn't go into Sandhurst? They were taking them absolutely free and without an exam and I'm sure old Bobby Sawyer would have nominated him.

'I'm going to stop now,

'Ever yr loving son, Billy.'[2]

The new aerodrome to which William referred in this letter was Bailleul. No. 4 moved there on 21 April, RFC units in the Ypres sector being regrouped as the tempo of the land battle increased. On Saturday, 8 May, the whole of the British Army's V Corps, under General Sir H. C. O. Plumer, came under heavy bombardment, the fire gradually being concentrated along the sector occupied by the 28th Division. A follow-up attack forced the infantry to fall back and between 11.00 hours and noon intense German troop movements were reported by RFC observers. Most of it was towards the Front and made up of ambulance wagons on their way to stand-by positions for the expected evacuation of casualties. Later in the afternoon and evening the general movement, no less intensive, was away from the Front, but British counter-attacks made throughout the day failed to recover the lost ground.

Among No. 4 Squadron members aloft on reconnaissance that afternoon was William, who had a lucky escape when an anti-aircraft shell burst close to his BE2c. He felt a blow in his right forearm; ignoring it he signalled the pilot to continue the flight, but when he realized that he was bleeding heavily their patrol was curtailed and the aeroplane returned to Bailleul. Robinson was quickly admitted to No. 7 Stationary Hospital, where two pieces of shrapnel were removed, and thence despatched to Boulogne, there to be informed he was sailing for England with one month's leave. Only later was it discovered that an 1806 halfpenny, which he kept in his left breast pocket for luck, was severely bent, having apparently deflected a stray piece of shrapnel.[3]

By 14 May, Robinson was in London, staying with his sister Grace at No. 76 Park Hill, Clapham, from where he light-heartedly wrote to allay his mother's fears:

'My darling old Mater,

'As you see I am home once again! How happy I am to be out of it for a bit. I came home last Wednesday — quick work wasn't it? At any rate it shows you how slightly I was wounded. I got it in the right forearm — a shrapnel bullet and very small piece of shell — and I am able to write already.

'It was about 4.50 am on Saturday over Lille that the beasts got me – I thought I was only bruised at first and went on with my reconnaissance, but after a bit my arm got a bit stiff and the blood dirtied all my maps, so we cut our reconnaissance short at the end and went back to the aerodrome. From there I went to the dressing hospital, where they took out the shrapnel bullet and dressed the wound and sent me off to Boulogne. I arrived there late Saturday night and was told I should probably go to England – great was my joy!

'So to cut a long tale short, here I am in dear old peaceful England. Dear old G came to see me at the hospital on Wednesday and brought me back here. Never was I more pleased at seeing old G – and never was I so absolutely happy as now. It only wants you dear old people for my happiness to be absolutely complete.

'I'm not going to write about the war, mother, all I'll say is it's dreadful and believe me when I say the Flying Corps get by *much* the best time and not half so many risks as the poor trench men.

'The doctor has given me a month's leave and you will bet I mean to make the most of it. When G leaves this house at the end of May, I mean to go to Boscombe to dear old Lady A. I'm going to write to her today about it – that reminds me, I've got hundreds of letters to write, so I'm going to stop now mother darling – I don't feel in a writing mood.

'Ever your loving son,

  Billy.

'My name is in the Roll of Honour today. Ha!'[4]

Having enjoyed his brief spell of convalescence, Robinson's next posting was to South Farnborough, where he reported for duty on 29 June to commence flying training, making his maiden flight under instruction the following day. On 18 July Robinson went solo for the first time, and a mere ten days later, flying a Maurice Farman, he qualified for Royal Aero Certificate No. 1475, having received just three hours and 26 minutes of tuition. Robinson was then sent to the RFC's Central Flying School based at Upavon in Wiltshire for a course of advanced training, arriving there on 14 August. Following four days spent 'settling in' Robinson, flying BE8 No. 693, made a 20-minute local flight, reaching a height of 1200 feet over the aerodrome. He was to fly a number of different aeroplanes at Upavon, including BE8s, BE8as, Caudrons and Martinsyde S.1 single-seaters.

Meanwhile William's brother Harold was spending a less exciting war at the 101st Grenadier's depot at Jubbulpore in northern India. On 18 September, 1915, he wrote to Irene:

'The depot work here is fairly heavy, for so many lists of clothes, belongings, etc., of casualties from East Africa have to be checked and tabulated. Then auctions have to be arranged and letters sent to relatives of the Sepoys as to what has to be done with the proceeds. I get most of this to do, as the depot commander, an awfully nice chap called Beaumont (capt.) does all the office work of the present regiment, *i.e.*, men and recruits who are in training here!'

William Braham Robinson (William Leefe Robinson's grandfather), the only son of Abraham Robinson, who served in the Royal Navy and spent 11 years as a French prisoner of war at Verdun. In 1869 Braham was appointed Master Shipwright and Engineer of HM Dockyard, Portsmouth; retiring in 1881, he went to live in Westwood Park, Southampton. (MRS R. DAVID)

Braham's wife Caroline Portch, née Sturgess. Their granddaughter Elsie Scott had fond memories of Caroline: 'I remember her at Southampton when she was over 80, feeding the chickens, gardening, getting up on the steps to prune the climbers and being called down to come in and make the pastry . . .' (MRS R. DAVID)

Caroline bore Braham Robinson seven children, among them Horace, who grew into a man of 'great compassion and charm'. Horace married Elizabeth Leefe in 1882, two years after the death of his first wife Alice, and the newly-weds made their home in India, where Horace owned a coffee estate. (MRS R. DAVID)

Elizabeth Leefe and Minnie Fisher (at left) strike informal poses for The Brompton Photographic Studio cameraman during the late 1870s. Elizabeth, known affectionately as Bessie to her husband, family and friends, would bear Horace seven children, the youngest, William, being born on 14 July, 1895, at Pollibetta. (MRS R. DAVID)

Horace Robinson stands on the wide verandah of the family bungalow at the Kaima Betta Estate in Pollibetta, South Coorg — seated in the foreground is the Robinson's eldest son Ernest. Although undated this rare photograph is though to have been taken around the turn of the century. (MRS R. G. LIBIN)

The only known photograph showing all of Horace and Bessie's children together — from left to right: Ruth, Katherine, Harold, Grace, William, Ernest and Irene. This delightful portrait, dated April 1900, was taken by Mentors of Bournemouth when the family were residing at their home at Boscombe. (MRS R. DAVID)

The Robinsons' four daughters were attractive youngsters as this April 1897 studio portrait reveals. Ruth (seated), Irene, Katherine and Grace became popular members of the community and rode almost everywhere on bicycles. To this day the 'bicycle pioneers' are recalled by members of 'The Bamboo Club' in Pollibetta. (MRS R. DAVID)

Horace Robinson at Kaima Betta with the family dog Niger. After World War I Horace and Bessie stayed on in Pollibetta until the early 1920s, when they left India for good and sailed to England, there to live in Wallington, Surrey, for the remainder of their lives. (MRS. R. DAVID)

Harold and Willie at Wandsworth sometime in 1903. The photograph was probably taken in the garden of their uncle, Dr Mark Robinson, from whose house, Geraldine Lodge in Geraldine Road, Wandsworth, London, was run a busy medical practice. The Robinson children often spent holidays there. (MRS R. DAVID)

Bishop Cotton School in Bangalore, India, where the Robinson children received part of their early education. William and Harold enrolled here in 1903 following initial schooling in England at The Dragon School, Oxford. Former 'BCS' pupils remembered Billy as being 'always full of mischief'. (MRS R. DAVID)

Horace Robinson and his daughter Grace outside their Kaima Betta bungalow. Members of 'The Bamboo Club', Pollibetta, established in 1886 to provide entertainment for, 'European planters that dominated coffee cultivation after the annexation of Coorg by the British Raj', hold fond memories of the Robinsons to this day. (MRS R. DAVID)

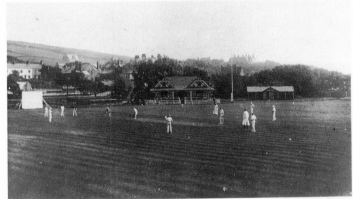

During September 1909 Harold and William Leefe Robinson enrolled at St Bees School on the coast of Cumberland, now Cumbria, where they were to complete their education. One of the many postcards they sent to their family in India included this view of the school's cricket field. (MRS R. DAVID)

A weekend picnic in Cumberland. William (third from right) and Harold Robinson (right) relax with some of their friends during a welcome break from studies at St Bees. By all accounts, the boys enjoyed their schooldays, were model pupils and both became heads of Eaglesfield House. (MRS R. G. LIBIN)

During the St Bees school holidays, William and Harold often stayed with relatives and this, undated, photograph was probably taken at Wandsworth with the family of Dr Mark Robinson. William is seated second from left and Harold at extreme right in this delightfully candid portrait. (Mrs R. G. Libin)

St Bees rugby team, date unknown; William Leefe Robinson is seated second from left in the second row. William became a useful member of the First XV and enjoyed all forms of sport, in which he invariably excelled. St Bees still proudly cherishes his rugger cap. (Mrs R. G. Libin)

During late August and early September of 1912, Harold and William, reunited with three of their sisters, spent a memorable holiday in Russia. They stayed here, at Berghof, a large house owned by Baroness von der Recke, where Katherine was giving English and piano lessons to the Recke children. (Mrs R. David)

*Russian summer holidays, 1912.
Harold and William stand behind
Frau von Stizk, May Recke and
Katherine Robinson in the
grounds of Berghof. William
termed the holiday as a 'huge
success' and both boys had been
shown great affection by the
baroness during their extended
visit.* (MRS R. G. LIBIN)

*One for the Berghof holiday album. In the back row are Harold, Daisy Pahlen, William and
Nickie Pahlen; seated (at left) is Baroness von der Recke, next to her Baroness Lille draws a bead
on the cameraman, whilst to her left sit Frau von Stizk and May Recke.*
(MRS R. G. LIBIN)

Back at St Bees both Harold and William resumed their studies with vigour following their extended Russian holiday. In April 1913 their sister Irene visited Cumberland, staying at Little Braithwaite Farm, where Harold probably took this delightful photograph. Irene returned to India a few weeks later. (Mrs R. David)

A handsome young man — William Leefe Robinson aged 18. This photograph was taken on 11 May, 1913, by Forsters of Whitehaven. Writing to Irene from St Bees, Harold enclosed the snap which William signed 'your ever-loving brother Willie', adding the wry comment, 'Don't I look soft!' (Mrs R. David)

In 1913 William had his first taste of 'military' service, attaining the rank of sergeant in the St Bees Officers' Training Corps. He is seen here, nearest the camera in the front row, at Mytchett, near Aldershot, Hampshire during manoeuvres. The following year he entered Sandhurst. (Mrs R. G. Libin)

Following five months at Sandhurst's Royal Military College, William Robinson was gazetted to the Worcester Regiment and posted to the Fifth Militia Battalion at Fort Tregantle, Cornwall, with the rank of second lieutenant. With the chance of early deployment to France unlikely William soon applied for other postings. (MRS R. G. LIBIN)

On 25 February, 1916, the husband of William's sister Grace, Arthur Limnell Robinson, a second lieutenant in the Northamptonshire's Eighth Battalion, died of wounds received on the Western Front during the Battle of Mons. This photograph of the couple was taken in January 1916 at Looe, Cornwall. (Mrs R. David)

Harold Robinson entered service with the Indian Army Regiment Overseas commissioned as a lieutenant with the 101st Grenadiers and based, initially, at Jubbulpore. He later served in Mesopotamia and participated in the ill-starred relief attempt at Kut-el-Amara in April 1916, during which he was fatally wounded. (Mrs R. David)

'Hors de combat'. Having successfully gained a transfer to the Royal Flying Corps in March 1915 as an observer with No. 4 Squadron, William Robinson was soon in action. On 7 May, 1915, during a reconnaissance over Lille he was struck in the arm by shrapnel. (Mrs R. G. Libin)

After convalescence Robinson was posted to South Farnborough on 29 June, 1915, to commence flying training. The following month he was at the Central Flying School, Upavon, Wiltshire, making his first solo flight there in BE8 693 (seen here later in its career) on 15 August. (J. M. BRUCE/G. S. LESLIE COLLECTION)

On 6 September, 1915, Robinson flew a Martinsyde Scout for the first time, taking aloft 4240 at 18.30 hours for a 15-minute flight over the Upavon aerodrome. Robinson's log book reveals he reached 1500 feet and that he made two attempts at landing. (J. M. BRUCE/G. S. LESLIE COLLECTION)

On 20 September, 1915, Lieutenant Robinson RFC joined No. 19 Squadron at Castle Bromwich, Birmingham. On 23 October at 11.00 hours he took BE2b 746 on a 30-minute flight from Farnborough. This photo shows the machine in France a few weeks previously. (J. M. BRUCE/G. S. LESLIE COLLECTION)

Robinson seated in an early production BE2c — note the aeroplane's wire wing trailing edges. Although the other officers are unidentified it is thought this photograph was probably taken at Castle Bromwich in late 1915; further details are lacking. (MRS R. DAVID)

BE2c 2693, fully equipped for night fighting, seen here at RNAS Eastchurch prior to its transfer to B Flight, No. 39 Home Defence Squadron RFC, at Suttons Farm, near Hornchurch, Essex. It was in this aeroplane that William Leefe Robinson brought down the German airship SL11. (J. M. Bruce/G. S. Leslie Collection)

The cockpit of 2693 included a rack for a three Lewis gun drums, and beneath this two large brass buttons which operated the Holt landing flares, one on each lower wing tip. Also of interest is the collapsible windscreen with its fabric-covered sides.
(J. M. Bruce/G. S. Leslie Collection)

In this view of 2693's cockpit may be noted three brass switches on the starboard side, together with a mass of wiring, relating to the aeroplane's night-flying equipment and most likely operating the wing tip and tail navigation lights. A rack of signal cartridges is situated beyond the control column. (J. M. BRUCE/G. S. LESLIE COLLECTION)

Hauptmann *Wilhelm Schramm when in the service of the Second* Eisenbahn *(Railway)*
Regiment during 1905-10. He subsequently entered the German Army Airship Division and
ultimately commanded several ships; his last was SL11 *in which he was to lose his life over*
London on 3 September, 1916. (P. AMESBURY)

On 5 October, 1912,
Wilhelm Schramm made
his first flight to
Königsberg as
commander of the non-
rigid Parseval P.III. This
celebratory postcard bore
a short message: 'After
splendid flight (in) P.III,
Berlin-Königsberg, 360
km in 7 hours, best
wishes W. Schramm.'
Hauptmann
Sommerfeldt and
Hauptmann von
Wobeser autographed the
card for good measure.
(P. AMESBURY)

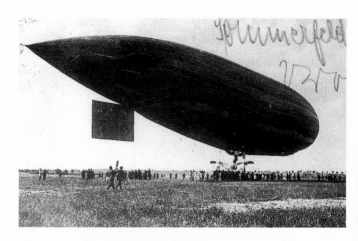

Officers and crew of the
Army Zeppelin LZ93.
The only personnel who
can be positively
identified are seated in
the front row: Leutnant
Vohdin at extreme left
and Hauptmann
Wilhelm Schramm
second from left.
Schramm took command
of LZ93 on 23 February,
1916. (MARINE
LUFTSCHIFFER
KAMERADSCHAFT)

This is the only known authenticated
photograph of SL11, showing the airship over
Hameln in August 1916, the picture being taken
by Wilhelm Schramm's elder brother, Otto.
Wilhelm often flew over Hameln and dipped his
airship's nose over the town to the delight of his
relatives living there. (P. AMESBURY)

In lighter vein, Harold continued:

'... Mrs Beaumont is an awfully nice girl and about your age, Rene, and I have some good fun with her. That reminds me of a yarn I told mother. I was up one day calling and (Mrs Beaumont) promptly took the responsibility of advising me what to wear at a coming Fancy Dress at the club given by the Commissioner. In the middle of it I rather think her stays must have broken, for she retired immediately in a room adjoining, and the clicking noise that proceeded from that direction seem to indicate to my inexperienced mind the idea of broken stays! When she came back five minutes later, she was quite cross at my reminding her that she had not yet decided on my fancy costume, at which she replied that she had better things to think of.

'But what amused me and made me laugh was dear old Mum's reply. "My dear Harold, *never* refer to such things as *stays*. We always call them *corsets*. Now do remember this my dear. Possibly she misunderstood you when in saying goodbye, you inadvertently said what lovely stays they were, instead of lovely weather."

'Perhaps Rene old thing, this is rather an indelicate subject to dwell upon, but this puts me in mind of what Bill once said to Miss Edison at St Bees when she was on one of her many visits to Mr and Mrs Burnett at Eaglesfield House. I remember it was at tea and she coquettishly said to Bill that she feared her visits were very frequent. "Yes, Miss Edison, no doubt, but then I notice that when you *do* come, your stays are always so short."

'I'm certain she understood then, though Bill's innocent face might have deceived her ...'[5]

The same day that Harold penned this letter, his brother was appointed flying officer and seconded following the gaining of the coveted 'wings' on the 15th. Five days later Robinson joined the strength of No. 19 Squadron at Castle Bromwich near Birmingham then under the command of Captain R. M. Rodwell. On 11 November, William wrote at length to Coorg:

'My darling Mother,

'Sunday round again – how the weeks seem to fly, a good many have flown too since I wrote you last, but don't think for a moment, darling old things at KB, that I don't think of you. Often do I come back here to my billet after a tiring day's work and think of dear old KB and its inmates – morbid sentiment? Perhaps, I confess I am often sentimental – but I consider to indulge in the right kind of sentiments are more helpful than harmful to one. Talking of sentiment, do you know the poems of Ernest Dowden? His whole life as well as his works was sentimental, morbidly so, yet I think some of his short poems are gorgeous. Poor old pater would not sympathise much with him, ruined by a woman and drink!

'Now for answering your last letter. You have just heard I have "got my Wings" – that is some time ago now. Ever since I've been here I've been acting as flight commander (a captain's place) and second in command of the squadron. The major went away for ten days some time ago and I was then left in charge of the whole squadron. You should have seen the other subs come up and salute me and ask my permission for various things — it was quite amusing. I had orderlies rushing about all day after and for me, not to mention the car and motorcycle at my disposal. However, I'm flight commander again now — and I have plenty to do with that alone what with about five machines and about 35 men under me. I am also squadron photography officer and wireless officer, added to which my machines are the only ones which carry machine guns, so they and their fittings have to be looked after.

'My dear old mother don't please praise me. I really don't deserve it, and at any rate I'm conceited enough as it is, and you'll only make me unsufferably so. (You see my spelling is still appalling, but I'm not going to use a dictionary writing home!) Now I'm going to give you an example of my abominable conceit. The other day it was most awfully windy and I was the only flying officer in the squadron who was allowed to go up — I took a passenger too — what do you think of a pilot who can pilot a machine and passenger through a 45 mile-an-hour gale!

'You seem to think whenever I go to town or anywhere I must be on leave — not at all. I go "on duty". I have delivered and brought machines to and from Farnborough, Northolt (Harrow) and various other places, and between times I manage to have a peep at "town" and my various "friends" there. Whenever I land I have a simply *ripping* time. I landed for lunch near Banbury the other day — you are immediately surrounded by people offering you cars, lunch, tea, bed and the Lord knows what not. Of course, if you are wise you generally pick out the grounds of a country house or large villa of some kind to land in. My last landing was made at Kenilworth. I had a passenger with me and we had the time of our lives. Talk about autograph books and cameras. By gad I was positively sick of seeing and signing my own signature. When I swore I would not sign another book one girl caught hold of my machine and said she would not leave go till I signed. So after much amusing argument I told her to give me the book, whereupon I placed my filthy hand, writing, "The mark of an aviator, W. L. Robinson" over the top of the hand mark. (My hand was all dirty with the oil from the engine.) The girl I liked best of all was a *sweet* little Flapper of about 17 called Kathleen Lennox, for whom I drew an aeroplane. Another girl lent me her camera with which I took some photographs — she developed them and has just sent me some prints. We stayed in Kenilworth two days and a night!!!!'[6]

Another letter soon followed:

Friday, 10 December, 1915

'Well, it's about time I wished you all the happiest of Happy Christmases and this I do with all my heart.

'Oh, what hundreds of things have happened since I last wrote. However, not time now, I must hurriedly finish off this scrawl. One rather funny thing happened the other day in Town.

'I had just finished tea at the Hotel Cecil and was feeling very pleased with myself in my double-breasted coat and Wings, when I noticed two girls looking curiously at me. They came up as if to speak to me then went away, evidently thinking better of it. I am not particularly slow on these occasions. I bounded after them and found myself saying in my sweetest (?) manner, "forgive my abominable impertinence if I am wrong, but have I not met you somewhere before?" Of course I was perfectly certain I had not, but that's a detail. They smiled – I had won.

'"As a matter of fact I was going to address you as Mr *Hamel*", said the eldest one. "You are exactly like him, if I may be so rude as to say so, I knew him awfully well, are you his brother?"

'*That* was the beginning (and) they were both ripping girls – and we have had quite nice times together!!

'Of course the introduction to the girls was quite ordinary; but it *is* strange about my likeness to Hamel. At Farnborough, the CFS and here I have met people who say I'm awfully like that gentleman – I'm sure it's very flattering.[7]

'I have just got your letter dated Nov 18th. The account of Allan Jackson's accident amused me greatly – my darling old mother those are quite every day occurrences, but believe me if you keep your head and are anything like a pilot you are *quite* safe. So he is taking observers up is he? Well I have three observers and several flyers to instruct in my flight. I take passengers up every day. Last Tuesday (7 December) I was to take an observer to Gosport (other side of the river to Portsmouth). We got as far as Oxford when the weather – wind, rain and fog – got so bad that we had to land. We saw a machine already on Port Meadow, so I landed there too, the other machine turned out to be one which my best friend here was also taking to Gosport.[8]

'To short a long story we had an A1 time in Oxford. Got the local Police and volunteers to guard the machines. Put up at the Mitre Hotel, went to the theatre and enjoyed ourselves generally. We were followed about most of the time by a band of small boys who would insist on cheering every now and then.

'Next morning the sky was perfect – and we decided to go on our way via Farnborough, where we would "fill up" our petrol and oil tanks.

'I flew fairly high, touching nearly 9000 feet – as luck would have it my engine began missing – I knew exactly what the matter was but could not remedy it in the air.[9] The poor observer, a fellow who had only been in an aeroplane about once before in his life, grew quite nervous – he kept on passing back notes to me. "The front part of the machine is vibrating horribly"; "what is the matter with the engine"; "will she hold out till we get to Farnborough", etc., etc. I laughed like anything at him, made a long nose and put out my tongue at him for reply. (You can't hear each other speak of course.) Once or twice I held up my hands to show I wasn't holding anything – I thought the poor man would have a fit. Anybody who knew the least little bit about flying would know we were as safe as a rock. I then shut off the engine and did a long glide of about six miles into Farnbrough aerodrome. I had the machine mended; waited a day for the weather to clear (during which time I went up to town and saw G and Kitty) then got fed up and returned back here, arranging for another pilot to deliver the machine to Gosport.

'I don't suppose a word of what I've written is sense – but I'm hurrying through this – I must be off.

'A Merry Christmas to you old Pekinese Pups and all.

'Ever your loving son,

Billy.'[10]

On Christmas Eve 1915 Robinson arrived at Joyce Green aerodrome, the base of No. 10 Reserve Aeroplane Squadron, having been 'lent' by his squadron commander to the London defence for operations against German airships, whose night-time raids on the country, virtually unopposed, had so incensed the British public. At noon on 24 January, Robinson made a trial flight in BE2c 4147, arriving over the South Farningham landing ground near Dartford, Kent, at 12.20 hours. Robinson had already made several night flights at Castle Bromwich and was fast becoming familiar with the risks and dangers associated with them. It was valuable training for Robinson and other officers who were part of Sir David Henderson's defence scheme, which involved a pair of BE2c biplanes (converted to single-seater fighters), their pilots, six mechanics and a detachment of Royal Engineers manning a searchlight on each of ten grounds encircling London. In the short period the pilots were based at South Farningham they were comfortably billeted in the Lion Hotel:

'My darling Mother,

'. . . This is a funny address isn't it? Well to cut a very long tale short I've been "lent" by my Birmingham squadron to the London Defence and here I am 18 miles east of the city and five miles out of Dartford, tucked away here with another pilot, some mechanics and two aeroplanes for the purpose of "Strafing Zepps" when they come this way.

'The other pilot (who by-the-way was with me learning to fly at Farnborough) and myself are living in this sweet little country hotel, all on our own – we are awfully comfortable here and the job is really a very slack one, we are chosen for it because we are supposed to be able to fly by night, an accomplishment which not every pilot can boast of I may state.

'There are only 20 aeroplanes on the London defence, but we are absolutely the first to receive the enemy should they come over. Now for heaven's sake don't get nervous mother, the job is quite safe if one has plenty of confidence.

'We had a visit from our general the other day – he's an awfully decent old boy and said my squadron commander had been worrying him to let me go back to his squadron, so I don't know if I'll stay here long I'm sure.

'The gentry about here are awfully decent. We have already been out to dinner, teas galore and have invitations for lunch. We are on duty day and night, but are allowed to go away for a few hours off to do a little shopping in town. I went to Endsleigh Palace Hospital and had a nice little chat with G. They gave us quite a decent lunch then tea. I say, mother, Mr Mockray (I know that's wrong, but I haven't the vaguest how to spell it) seems to have piled it on a bit thick about me. I'm sure I'm really the most appalling specimen of humanity both morally and physically.

'By-the-by you might thank pater for his last "letter" – which consisted of a few words written on the face of a bill to the effect that if the bill went astray he wishes me to pay it promptly. The date of the bill was all wrong as it happened to be trousers and knickers which I had made for me at Sandhurst and which I thought was included in my Sandhurst kit – however that's that.

'So sleepy, so with belated but hearty wishes of luck and happiness throughout 1916 and all following years with love to all.

'I remain your ever loving son.

Billy the Birdman.'[11]

Robinson remained at South Farningham until 12 January, 1916, having been recalled to Castle Bromwich by his commanding officer. Thanks to the poor weather the return flight was a protracted one and it was not until some days later that Robinson returned to Birmingham, as a letter to his mother on 6 February outlined:

'My darling Mother,

'G has just sent on your letter dated 12th of Jan. I can't say father's letter which came at the same time greatly cheered me up. He talks of my neglect of an obvious *duty* by not writing every mail – it's the least a *good* son can do – and so on and so forth. All this may or may not be the truth, but you can tell father from me that it is certainly *not* the best way of getting round his youngest son, or convincing him of his obvious *duty*. After this testy introduction he goes on to say that now I have good pay he hopes I will fulfil my promise (?) at once and pay £5 into his deposit order a/c at the A and N stores and, he *hopes* that he shall not have to refer to this matter again! I will write out a check for the sum at once . . .[12]

. . . 'Oh, I must stop, but my darling old mother you can't think what a mood pater's notes put me in, when they are in this strain. It makes me wild, when he suggests for a minute that my love for the best mother and home on God's earth is fading. Is love measured by the number – let alone the importance – of letters written *per* month or year? I am not pretending to defend my negligence – for neglect I willingly admit it is. But the attitude of righteous indignation father adopts, and the "essays" on duty he sends one, are not calculated to improve matters or make one take the right attitude about things. Father says you "spoil" us children, because, I suppose, you don't demand our love, but simply foster it, well. But I *will* stop, I have *no right* to write all this.

'Well, my darling mother it would be impossible to tell you all that has happened since I last wrote. I believe you heard I had gone to a little country place called Farningham, where I had simply the time of my life. Another pilot and myself were on London defence and were absolutely on our own, billeted in a small country hotel. Well, my squadron commander made such a fuss about having me back at Birmingham, that I was recalled. The day after arriving back at Castle Bromwich, I was sent off to Newcastle to fly a new kind of machine down to the Central Flying School, Salisbury Plain, a distance of about 350 miles by air.

'I was going to do it in one day, just calling at Birmingham for petrol, but fate decreed otherwise. I ended up by staying four days in Newcastle owing to the machine not being quite ready and the weather being very bad. I forgot to tell you I had brought a friend up with me as he wanted the ride back to Birmingham. We didn't waste our time in Newcastle and really had a very good time. There are no RFC people there so my little side cap and Wings was greatly admired. It is really quite amusing to go into a hotel or café, and people turn round and nudge one another, and you often hear, "Royal Flying Corps", "Flying man", etc., etc., in awed whispers and, "Oh, what a nice flying boy" and so on from the coarser class of female. We managed to get friendly with two awfully decent men, one the kind of boss of the aeroplane works here, and the other in charge of the huge gun factory. We spent a great deal of time going all over the works.

'They told us a secret about a big gun they had there which will apparently astonish the world. Fancy, they turn out six complete batteries with fittings and all every week – that is counting the guns alone, 36 guns. The works were really wonderful and awfully interesting.

'The Armstrong Whitworth aeroplane works were so full of interest to one like myself who takes such an interest in that line of engineering.

'We were ready to start at last on the Wednesday,[13] that is a week ago last Wednesday. It was interesting flying a machine I knew no one but the testers had flown before – it is quite *the* latest Armstrong.[14] It does about 94 miles an hour (relative to the air of course) which is really very fast considering its size and carrying power. I got off in grand style – though I'm afraid the passenger was a bit nervous to start with, but I soon made him change his expression by making faces at him, laughing and generally playing the fool.

'We hadn't been aloft for quite an hour when we got into rather dense fog – having been caught in a fog before I looked for a landing ground, noticed quite a nice country house, and came down near it. To make a long story short, we were put up in the country house, which happened to belong to a Mr Fairfax, a descendant of the Lord Fairfax of Cromwell and Civil War fame. He was an eccentric old fellow getting on for 50 but with a charming young wife of not much over 20 – it was a lovely old house furnished in the most gorgeous old style. They treated us most awfully well and the pretty young wife was simply sweet. We had a gorgeous room with a butler to come in and brush and fold our clothes in the morning – everything was done so perfectly and expensively.

'The whole countryside turned out next morning when we started off. By-the-by the name of the place was Bilborough, quite a tiny village about five miles from York. In a minute or two we were at York, and I came down for a fill up of petrol, after which we meant if possible to go straight on to Upavon. But no luck and we ran into more mist just after leaving Doncaster. This time I lost my whereabouts completely. I cruised about, came down and ran into thick black smoke – it *was* filthy. There is only one town which could give off such smoke as this thought I – and that is Sheffield. It was – I had unknowingly drifted far too much to the right (*i.e.*, west) and I was in the black country. I steered to a clearer patch in the sky, came down, and I must say with great skill, landing in what I found out to be Chesterfield, a largish town 12 miles from Sheffield.

'We stayed at this place two days and two nights and were entertained by the people belonging to a hospital nearby, although we actually slept and had breakfast at the Station Hotel! The second night we took the matron and an awfully charming, young and pretty girl doctor to Sheffield, where we "did" supper and a ripping theatre.

'On Saturday morning following, we left, after writing our names in autograph albums, imposing our beaming visages to the camera and bidding tender farewells – arriving at Birmingham about an hour later.

'I wanted to see a friend in Birmingham on Sunday, so we didn't go to the CFS till the Wednesday. We did the journey from Birmingham to Salisbury Plain in about an hour and a half, which isn't so bad considering I went to Oxford, where I landed at Port Meadow and thereby amused a number of subalterns in training there.

'I came back to Birmingham the same night (Monday), but as I went straight to my billet I heard nothing about the Zepp raid till the next morning.[15]

'I then went straight off on the London Zepp-Strafing job at Croydon – and the next day (Wednesday) was shunted off here – one of the outer circle of London defence stations.

'There are only two of us night pilots here with two mechanics kept in tents in a large grass field. We are supposed to go up in case of day or night attack (especially the last, as we are supposed to be trained night pilots). If there are no scares we are supposed to fly our machines twice a week to see if they are working alright. Today being a lovely day I went up, mucked about a bit, looped-the-loop four times and came down. Now don't for heaven's sake get nervous when I tell you I loop-the-loop – it's the easiest and safest thing to do in the world in the machines you have got. Trust me, my darling mother, not to do anything rash.

'By-the-way I found out the other day that two of my squadron commanders have put me up *three* times for promotion between them – who is preventing my promotion I can't think, but there must be someone, or else it would have gone through ages ago.

'Hornchurch is a quaint old little village just north of the Thames and 12 miles from Town – in fact about just opposite my old station, Farningham. I and the other pilot take it in turns to go up to Town once or twice a week in the daytime – although of course we can never stay a night there. I went up the other morning and spent the day with my friend Ridley, who was at Farningham with me, he is really an awfully nice chap and has got *four* charming sisters.

'Well, mother, good-night I'm sleepy – let's hope I dream of all you darling old K-Bites and the old place itself. Father, if you see this letter forgive what I wrote in the first part, I know you would if I could only grip your hand.

'Ever your loving son,

   Billy.'[16]

Four days prior to penning the first part of this letter Robinson had arrived at Hornchurch near the landing ground at Suttons Farm, where one of the elements of the newly-formed No. 19 Reserve Aeroplane Squadron was situated. On 4 February Robinson made his first flight from the aerodrome in BE2c 4110, testing the biplane's tail incidence gear. Weeks of training and night-flying ensued, but it would not be until 25 April that William Leefe Robinson had his first encounter with one of Germany's Zeppelin bombers.

CHAPTER FOUR

ZEPPELINS OVER ENGLAND

When the attacks on London, in the autumn of 1915, revealed the complete ineffectiveness of the defences, Lord Kitchener had sent for Sir David Henderson. 'What are you going to do about these airship raids?' he had asked, to which the Director-General of Military Aeronautics replied that the responsibility rested with the Royal Naval Air Service. 'I do not care who has the responsibility,' Lord Kitchener retorted. 'If there are any more Zeppelin raids and the Royal Flying Corps do not interfere with them, I shall hold you responsible.'

The War in the Air, Volume III, 1931

In 1899 the Hague Declaration was drawn up to prevent countries from launching projectiles or explosives from 'balloons or other kinds of aerial vessels'.[1] The restriction remained until 1907 when it came up for renewal, but from representatives of 44 countries only 27 added their names to the new agreement. Of the powers to be involved in the European war, four gave their support: Belgium, Great Britain, Portugal and the United States of America. But in any case the agreement automatically became void in August 1914 because of a proviso that restrictions would be lifted if, in the event of war between the contracting powers, one country was supported by one of those that had not signed previously.

An outcome of the Hague Conference was the Land War Convention, of which Article 25 was the only existing international rule prior to the outbreak of war that referred to air bombardment. It forbade the world powers from bombing undefended areas by 'any means whatsoever'[2] and was deliberately phrased to imply aerial attack. But it was unclear what constituted an undefended area, and Article 2 of the Naval Convention sought to clarify:

'Military works, military or naval establishments, depots of arms or war material, workshops or plant which could be utilized for the needs of a hostile fleet or army, and ships of war in the harbour are not included in this prohibition . . . A naval commander may destroy them with artillery, after a summons followed by a reasonable interval of time, if all other means are impossible, and when the local authorities have not themselves destroyed them within the time fixed.'³

During the same year as the second conference, the British Government became concerned over the development of Count Zeppelin's airships. The Anglo-German 'arms race' was at its peak by then and there were fears that Zeppelins would add marine reconnaissance and even bombing to their capabilities. A year later the Government formed a committee, chaired by Lord Esher, to enquire into the possible dangers to which the country could be subjected by the advance of aeronautics.

Prior to World War I Zeppelins had safely carried hundreds of passengers, remained airborne for over 24 hours, covered distances of up to 900 miles and were the centre of much exaggeration and sensationalism. Even before August 1914, many impressionable people in Great Britain reported seeing Zeppelins cruising along the coast, and rumours of German spies quickly spread. Such sightings were, of course, pure imagination, but the likely threat of bombardment was not one to be taken lightly. After war was declared the anticipated airship raids failed to materialize and it was German seaplanes operating from the French coast that made the first aerial attacks upon Great Britain. None of these sporadic incursions caused serious damage, but many people remained apprehensive about the 'Bloody Zepps'.

In September 1914 the staff of both the German Army and Naval Airship Divisions had debated the bombing of England, but at that time they were faced with a number of problems. Chief among these was that there were simply not enough airships, and it was agreed that air raids would have to wait, at least until the large number of ships then being built had entered service, something which would not transpire for several months. Secondly, both *Kaiser* Wilhelm and Chancellor Theobold von Bethmann-Hollweg were loath to sanction bombing of London, despite *Konteradmiral* Paul Behncke's arguments to the contrary. The 'Supreme War Lord' feared for the safety of his royal cousins, King George V and Queen Mary, and was also reluctant to allow his airship crews to damage any of London's historic buildings. ·

Eventually, after much wrangling within the German General Staff, matters came to a head. On 7 January, 1915, the Chief of the Naval Staff, *Admiral* Hugo von Pohl, demanded an audience with the *Kaiser*. Frequent badgering by his subordinates persuaded him to lay arguments before His Imperial Majesty in a last-ditch effort to obtain sanctions for air raids. The agenda stressed that only military buildings should be bombed − civilian homes were to be avoided if at all possible. It did not include co-operation with the Army Airship Division, this being considered impracticable and possibly postpone the navy's planned offensive.

After the meeting, von Pohl came away satisfied, and three days later wired to the Commander-in-Chief of the High Seas Fleet:

'Air attacks on England approved by Supreme War Lord. Targets not to be attacked in London, but rather docks and military establishments in the Lower Thames and on the English coast.'⁴

From 19 January, 1915, when the Naval Zeppelins *L3*, *L4* and *L6* set out on the first successful airship raid of the war, until 24 August the following year, 39 raids were mounted, resulting in the deaths of 439 people, and almost 980 casualties. During much of this period the 'Baby Killers' – as the Press were quick to dub the dreaded nocturnal raiders – carried out their attacks virtually unhindered by British defences, which for the early part of the war were seriously inadequate.

As a result of the first Zeppelin raids in January Captain Murray Seuter, of the Royal Naval Air Service, proposed rapid formation of a mobile anti-aircraft force, and although the Eastern Mobile Section with its high-angle machine guns, pom-poms and searchlights restored much public confidence, the guns' limited range made them generally ineffectual. As the months went by and the air raids continued so the number of guns increased; further aeroplane landing grounds were being established as both the Army and Navy argued as to with which of them lay the direct responsibility for the country's defences.

On 8 September, one of the German Naval Airship Division's most experienced and successful commanders, *Kapitänleutnant* Heinrich Mathy in the Zeppelin *L13*, made a highly destructive raid on London; in fact it proved to be the single most devastating attack by any German aeroplane or airship on the British Isles during the entire war. Mathy caused material damage amounting tó £534,387 of which £530,787 was the result of the great fires that raged in the capital following his 'almost leisurely' course over London. Twenty-two people were killed and many more injured. The raid incensed public opinion and the combined forces came in for bitter criticism, while German-born citizens and shopkeepers found themselves the targets of hatred and persecution as the raids continued:

'A woman was in the midst of a struggling mob; her blouse half-torn off, her fair hair fallen, her face contorted with pain and terror, blood running down her bare white arm. A big, drunken man flung her to the ground. She was lost to sight . . .'[5]

Eventually it was realized that the responsibility for London's defences should rest with *one* officer if the situation was to improve and on 12 September, 1916, Admiral Sir Percy Scott, a gunnery expert, was appointed to the task. Having obtained a 'free hand' from former First Lord of the Admiralty Winston Churchill, Scott wasted little time. The short-range pom-poms were replaced with 75 mm anti-aircraft guns mounted on trucks for mobility, while rapid expansion and re-organization of both Royal Flying Corps and Royal Naval Air Service defence units took place.

The RFC located two suitable areas of farmland near London for temporary landing grounds. One, occupying 90 acres, was Thomas Crawford's Suttons Farm in Essex, two miles from Hornchurch; the other, at 60 acres, was farmed by Mr W. Poulter and lay alongside the Chadwell Heath road. The lands were quickly requisitioned and officially became Temporary Landing Grounds II and III respectively.

Lieutenant Colonel W. G. Salmond, commanding the RFC's Fifth Wing, provided seven BE2c machines, one of them, together with an SE4, being sent to Joyce Green. The remaining six went in pairs to Hainault Farm, Northolt, and Suttons Farm, along with hangars, fuel and equipment.

Each night at the landing grounds, a pilot was on standby. If airships were seen approaching London, the War Office telephoned the hour at which the aeroplane was to take off. Sufficient lead time was calculated for the slow-climbing BE2c to reach 8000 feet, but if the pilot failed to make contact he was to land after 90 minutes, and in the event of bad weather the War Office was informed before the pilot stood down. Searchlights were placed near Becontree Heath and Chigwell Row, while two more were considered for Buckhurst Hill and Upminster. Subsequently, chains of observers were placed north-east of the landing grounds so that rockets could be sent up if airships were seen. The rockets were of different colours to denote the direction Zeppelins were taking, the colours previously notified to each pilot.

Within two days all the aeroplanes had been delivered, pilots and ground crew billeted, equipment installed, telephones connected and flight tests made. On 2 October, Lieutenant Jenkins from No. 14 Squadron and Second Lieutenant Yates of No. 23 flew into Suttons Farm and later that day Second Lieutenant John Slessor collected a new BE2c from the Daimler works and reported to Suttons Farm. On arrival he relieved Jenkins, who flew to Hainault Farm, bringing the flight there up to full strength.

The facilities at Suttons Farm were, to say the least, fairly primitive. The flare path was formed by two rows of petrol cans, their lids removed and crammed with a mixture of petrol, paraffin and cotton waste. Laid out in the shape of an L, with the shorter arm at the upwind end of the field, the flare path was 300 yards long: the airfield itself being only 500 yards square.

Pilots carried a Very pistol in their machines and prior to landing would fire a green light. If the flare path was clear, the ground crew also fired a green flare before the pilot landed. At that time no machine-guns were installed in the BE2cs, the idea being to attack the Zeppelins from above with 20 lb Hales bombs or batches of Ranken explosive darts.

On the night of 13 October, the last raid of 1915 resulted in the deaths of 71 people, the injury of nearly 130 more with thousands of pounds' worth of damage. Both *L15* (*Kapitänleutnant* Joachim Breithaupt) and *L13* (*Kapitänleutnant* Mathy) reached the capital and their bombs took a heavy toll. Five RFC aeroplanes had taken off from the temporary landing grounds, but only one of them, flown by 18-year-old John Slessor, managed to get anywhere near the enemy. To his frustration he was left standing as *L15* stuck her nose upwards and kept on climbing until well out of range.[6]

Once London had recovered from this latest attack there were further recriminations, the Government being vociferously blamed for its failure in protecting the civilian population. The waxing moon and the onset of winter reduced the activities of Germany's airship fleet for a while, giving both Admiralty and War Office breathing space to sort out their differences and finally establish an effective system.

By 26 October, the aeroplane defence of London had ceased to exist; while the fields remained War Office property the aeroplanes and men had returned to their units and thence to the Western Front and at Suttons Farm sheep returned to graze on their old field. Still the Army and Naval authorities could not reach a firm decision and a week passed before the Admiralty announced that while it had considered aeroplanes vital for

London's defence it had changed its attitude in the light of recent raids. Then another conference was arranged, and despite the absence of Kitchener (overseas in the Dardanelles) it was agreed that the RFC would be responsible for *all* inland air defence, while the RNAS supplied cover over the sea. The Army slowly gained control of London's guns and searchlights, while in December a pair of BE2cs with night-flying pilots were sent to each of ten airfields on permanent standby: Chingford, Croydon, Hainault Farm, Hendon, Hounslow, Joyce Green, Northolt, South Farningham, Suttons Farm and Wimbledon Common. Each field was maintained by six mechanics and a Royal Engineer party with a searchlight.

For a while, at least, harmony had been achieved, but it was short-lived. When Kitchener returned, having reviewed the situation overseas, he considered RFC expansion in France far more important than establishing a large number of permanent home defence stations and on 10 January, 1916, Kitchener ordered the Army to *reverse* its decision. Now Army gunners and searchlight teams would come under Admiralty control; not surprisingly the Navy was incensed and the two arms were still at loggerheads when at the end of the month a large force of Zeppelins made the first attack on the Midlands.

Despite the conflict between the two services, the War Office did make one important move following the raid on the Midlands. They appointed the experienced Major T. C. R. Higgins, the officer in command of No. 19 Reserve Aeroplane Squadron, to take control of all corps aerodromes around London and organize his own unit for the capital's defence.

On 10 February, the War Committee held another meeting and at last settled on a workable division of responsibility. The Admiralty would deal with airships approaching the coastlines while the Army would be in charge of all land defences and:

'. . . provide the aeroplanes required to work with the Home Defence troops and to protect garrisons and vulnerable areas and the Flying Stations required to enable their aircraft to undertake their duties.'[7]

Just under a week later the responsibility for London's defence passed to Field Marshal Lord French, Commander-in-Chief Home Forces; the entire country's defence eventually coming under his command. Initially a number of aeroplanes were to be permanently based near each defence area with additional machines in advance of those areas for mobile defence. Unfortunately the organization of home defence evolved slowly owing to shortage of personnel and equipment. One solution was to despatch three BE2cs each to training squadrons in the key areas of Doncaster, Dover, Norwich and Thetford; a further six to reinforce No. 5 Reserve Aeroplane Squadron in the defence of Birmingham and Coventry. All this had been completed by 1 March. For Leeds and Hull, No. 33 Squadron was to be moved to Bramham Moor from Bristol and No. 34 Squadron from Castle Bromwich to Beverley, near York. The latter move did not materialize and Hull's defence was initially provided by No. 47 Squadron (formed at Beverley on 1 March, 1916) and, later on, a detachment from No.33, which moved to Bramham Moor in April. The senior officer of each unit was responsible for ordering his pilots aloft on receipt of an air raid warning. The aeroplanes from each station made successive patrols at heights between 8000 and 10,000 feet above their own landing grounds, a normal patrol lasting two hours. A second machine was sent up after one and a half hours to ensure continuity.

Despite urgent requirements in France, March 1916 saw the requirement for home defence establishments being laid down as ten squadrons to be drawn from a total of 70 units sanctioned for the RFC in December 1915. In consequence several squadrons already formed or about to be formed in England were designated Home Defence Squadrons and at the same time the aeroplane defence of London was reorganized. All of London's RFC units were grouped together on 25 March, thenceforth being known as the 18th Wing. All the units involved, still called Reserve Aeroplane Squadrons, came under the command of Lieutenant Colonel Fenton Vesey Holt, recently returned from France. Eventually these particular detachments, hitherto under the control of No. 19 Reserve Aeroplane Squadron, became No. 39 Home Defence Squadron, on 15 April, 1916. The newly formed unit had its base at Hounslow, where a flight of six machines was sent along, with Higgins as overall commander. During May and June two more flights of six aeroplanes each were flown to Hainault and Suttons Farms. Soon afterwards a Home Defence Wing was formed and training duties were removed from home defence squadrons. Under the command of Holt and with its headquarters at Adastral House, the wing comprised No. 33 Home Defence Squadron at Bramham Moor, No. 36 at Cramlington, No. 38 formed at Castle Bromwich, No. 39 in the London area, No. 50 at Dover and No. 51 Squadron at Norwich. Six searchlights were installed at each home defence unit.

Another result of the shift of responsibility was the total revision of intelligence and warning organizations, both playing a major part in defence. When Rear Admiral Sir Reginald Hall became the Director of Intelligence in November 1914 he found that a select band of cryptographers under Sir Alfred Ewing was already intercepting German Navy wireless messages. Hall was to become a legendary figure in intelligence operations in World War I. Room 40, Old Building, at the Admiralty was where Hall's men were to receive and decode vital transmissions and then advise British forces accordingly. As the war progressed their work became ever more vital in keeping track of the Zeppelins as they made their nocturnal incursions.

On the night of 31 March/1 April, 1916, the reorganized defences scored their first success, as accurate anti-aircraft fire disabled Breithaupt's *L15*, which also came under spirited attack from Second Lieutenant Alfred de Bathe Brandon flying a BE2c out of Hainault Farm. Brandon managed to hurl a batch of explosive darts at the airship, which, due to loss of gas from ruptured cells, had been losing precious height, allowing the pilot a rare opportunity to get above one of the raiders. *L15* eventually came down on Margate Sands and was totally wrecked, although its crew, with the exception of one man who drowned, was captured unharmed.[8] Few members of the public saw the airship's demise, and although the British Press made much of the defence's first success it only seemed to partially appease civilians at large.

Another Zeppelin had been brought down on 7 June, 1915, as it returned to Belgium following a abortive raid on the British Isles. This was the Army's *LZ37* and it was blasted out of the sky by Sub-Lieutenant Reginald Alexander John Warneford, who successfully bombed it from above. For this exploit, the first time one of the 'Baby Killers' had been bested in the air, Warneford was awarded the Victoria Cross and his name became a household word all over the country. Ten days later he was dead, the victim of a flying accident.[9]

Small bombs were not the only form of weapons designed for use against Zeppelins; there were a number of alternatives, some of which were somewhat hair-raising. As well as a large number of weird and wonderful specially-designed anti-Zeppelin fighters, none of which was destined to see operational service, there was no shortage of ideas for destructive devices such as trailing aerial mines, a cordon of armed kite balloons around London and an early form of wire-guided missile. 'Fiery Grapnels' were exactly what their name suggested – an incendiary device fitted with large barbed hooks intended to snag and tear a Zeppelin's outer cover and ignite the escaping gas. The French *Le Prieur* rocket was officially issued to Home Defence units, and although successful in France against observation balloons, there is no record of them having been used against airships, several RFC squadron pilots defying orders and quietly removing the rockets, regarding them as useless deadweight. Ranken explosive darts were a variation on the 'Fiery Grapnel' theme, though much smaller devices, and carried in large batches inside the cockpit. Operational experience, however, was to prove that incendiary ammunition from an ordinary machine gun would be the most effective measure against the airships.

When Warneford had his first ever encounter with a Zeppelin (*LZ39* on 17 May, 1915) his observer had fired inconclusively at their giant adversary with a .45 rifle loaded with a new form of incendiary bullet designed to ignite the highly volatile hydrogen-filled gas cells inside the airship. At the time, it was thought the 'flaming bullets' had failed because the Germans used an inert gas 'wall' between the cells and the outer covering of their airships, a belief that was quite erroneous. The bullets failed because an insufficient amount of air was mixed with the hydrogen, thus preventing ignition; what was needed was some form of explosive bullet.

Early British experiments with tracer ammunition were discouraging, but in 1916 the Ministry of Munitions took over part of the Aerators Company's experimental factory. In June 1915, trials of a new tracing composition of one part magnesium to eight of barium peroxide were considered satisfactory, and after extensive tests the bullet was approved for immediate issue to the RFC. It was known as 'Sparklet', but was officially designated SPK Mk VIIT.

Chemist James Francis Buckingham was the proprietor of a small engineering works in Coventry. As early as 1914 Buckingham had foreseen the value of incendiary ammunition for use against airships and decided to sketch out some ideas for a new bullet. After several experiments he elected to use phosphorus and took out his first patent on 29 January, 1915. Three months later he demonstrated his .45 bullet before RNAS officers, and following successful destruction of test balloons at a range of 400 yards, was encouraged to improve the projectile. The result was a .303 version for use in machine-guns, and on 23 October the Admiralty were suitably impressed to place a firm contract for production.

On 27 April, the first contract from the Ministry of Munitions on behalf of the RFC was placed. Buckingham modified the shape to match Mk VII rounds and to ensure uniformity for mass production. On 24 June he patented his Mk VII bullet, which was used without modification for the rest of the war.

Buckingham's bullet consisted of a cupro-nickel 'envelope', which contained the phosphorus composition, with two lead plugs inserted, the first serrated and the second acting as base plug. Tapered at one end, this formed an annular cavity lining up with the side hole in the envelope, which was sealed with a fusible alloy that melted on firing, the base of the bullet being spun over and soldered. On firing, phosphor ran down the serrations in the first lead pellet into the annular space around the front of the second, whence it was ejected through the hole in the envelope, igniting on contact with the air. Over 26 million rounds of Buckingham were manufactured during the war.

In 1915 the bogus inert gas theory had persuaded Commander Francis Arthur Brock (in charge of the Intelligence Section of the Air Department of the Admiralty) to produce a bullet that would explode between gas cells and outer covering. He developed the design at his own expense, trials in October 1915 proving highly successful when the bullet was fired from a Lewis gun at short range. Later modifications increased the range to 800 yards, and in May 1916 an order for half a million Brock bullets was placed with Messrs C. T. Brock and Co Ltd, of Sutton. Despite some manufacturing problems, the order was completed by December, after which no more were ordered, since the bullets had been superseded early in 1917 for the RFC. The RNAS, however, used the Brock until the Armistice.

John Pomeroy, an Australian engineer, submitted his explosive bullet design to the War Office in August 1914, but as they were disinterested, he returned home. Following several trials in America Pomeroy came back to England in June 1915 and tried the War Office once again, but without success. Nevertheless, by December the Munitions Inventions Department took up Pomeroy's idea and carried out a series of trials; in May an order for half a million rounds was placed. While the bullet was being developed, the RFC expressed great interest and demanded large supplies, but problems arose. During mass production it was found that premature explosions were occurring because the composition was being 'nipped' between core and envelope. A copper tube or 'warhead' was inserted to cover the joint and the composition inside and the problem was solved. Trials undertaken in July gave satisfactory results, and the Pomeroy bullet, officially the PSA, was generally approved the following month. Towards the end of 1916 the bullet was improved to render it more sensitive, and the PSA Mk II bullet was accepted in February 1917, superseding the original issue. Only the RFC used the Pomeroy for home defence use. 'Sparklet', Buckingham, Brock or Pomeroy were to be rarely, if ever, used singly, but mixed in several combinations they promised to be deadly and just how deadly was soon to become apparent.

CHAPTER FIVE

NOCTURNAL ENCOUNTER

... At about 10.45 p.m. on the night of 25th inst., I received orders to patrol at 5000 feet. This I did and kept at 5000 feet for a few minutes, then decided to climb. When just over 7000 feet, I noticed a great number of searchlights pointing in a northerly direction; turning round I saw the Zeppelin. I at once turned and climbed in its direction. When just over 8000 feet, I was in a fairly good position to use my machine gun; this I did, firing immediately under the ship. The firing must have had little or no effect, for the Zeppelin must have been a good 2000 feet above me, if not more (by this time I was about 8000 feet) ...

Report of Patrol by Lieutenant W. L. Robinson,
26 April, 1916

When Major W. C. H. Mansfield took command of No. 39 Home Defence Squadron on 13 June, 1916, C Flight at Hainault Farm came under the command of Second Lieutenant Alfred Brandon, and Lieutenant William Robinson would ultimately take over B Flight at Suttons Farm, which comprised Lieutenants C. C. Brock, C. C. Durston, P. R. Mallinson, F. Sowrey and W. J. Tempest. 26 July saw the command of the squadron pass to Major A. H. Morton and, some time later, A Flight (Captain L. S. Ross) switched from Hounslow to North Weald Bassett, the headquarters being moved to Salway Lodge at Woodford Green.

Main equipment of the new squadrons was the Royal Aircraft Factory BE2c, an aeroplane that enjoyed widespread use with both the RFC and RNAS. Considerable numbers were built and while its initial service career was a great success (the BE being a superb reconnaissance vehicle) it was soon outclassed in France by superior German fighters. Yet the machine's slow speed and inherent stability, qualities which made it so vulnerable over the Western Front, made it the ideal night-fighter, providing a steady platform from which to unleash a wide variety of anti-Zeppelin devices. By early 1916 those aeroplanes issued to home defence units had been suitably modified 'in the field' in order to fulfil their new role.

Home defence BE2c machines were invariably flown as single-seaters, and experience soon showed that the slightly increased performance was offset by air suction, a result of the vacant front cockpit. Consequently this was covered with an aluminium panel secured by straps, to overcome the problem. Instrumentation for the pilot included an inclinometer, revolution counter, altimeter, airspeed indicator and a centrally-mounted compass fitted to a cut-out in the cockpit decking underneath the windscreen. Engine on/off switches were mounted outside the cockpit; internally, a pressure pump was fixed to the starboard side and a rudimentary throttle to port. A wooden control column and rudder bar carried the cables via control horns to ailerons, elevators and rudder, the cables often doubled as insurance against severance. On a basket-weave seat, the pilot sat swathed in protective leathers, his face smeared with whale oil to combat the cold, and secured with a wide safety strap around his midriff. There was no oxygen equipment, no radio, no cockpit heating and no parachute.[1]

For anti-Zeppelin duties the BE2c was variously armed with either four rack-mounted high-explosive bombs or one box containing 24 explosive darts, *Le Prieur* rockets on the outer interplane struts and/or an upward-firing Lewis machine gun with three to five drums of mixed ammunition; small lamps were mounted on the instrument panel and readings were daubed with 'radium'. Identification lamps were fitted to each wing tip, and below them, on special brackets, were Holt landing flares, which were electrically operated from two brass buttons in the cockpit. Such were the aeroplanes that Robinson and his fellow officers were to match against Germany's airship squadrons.

At Suttons Farm, wooden sheds of a more permanent nature were being constructed to replace temporary canvas 'RE5' hangars. Workshop facilities and living quarters, the latter converted from wooden aeroplane crates, began to appear on the farm, whilst Thomas Crawford and his son Tom continued to work what was left of the 385 acres that formed part of the Manor of Suttons. The large farmhouse was built on the very plot where the ancient manor house once stood, that having been acquired in 1392, together with the Manor of Hornchurch Hall, by William of Wykeham from the Monks of St Bernard and presented by him to St Mary de Winton College, Oxford. Truly an historic site.

Under Robinson, the officers and men of B Flight, No. 39 HDS, enjoyed a fairly relaxed and good-humoured existence. To his family it was either Willie, Billy or Bill, but to his fellow officers he was Robby or, more usually, Robin; he was greatly liked and respected by all those who came into contact with him:

'He had a remarkable gift for managing men, especially bad characters, and he endeared himself to all who served him. He was never out of temper or depressed, and wherever he was he diffused an air of confidence and hope. He managed to get the best out of everybody and won a general affection because he himself gave out so much of it.'[2]

Chief among Robinson's closest friends was Second Lieutenant Frederick Sowrey[3] and Captain Robert Sidney Stammers, whose young sister Vera accompanied the latter's fiancée on frequent visits to the squadron. Vera attended several pre-flight briefings, most of which were held around a card table just inside one of the hangars, and recalls that even at that time visitors to Suttons Farm were numerous:

'Weekend after weekend, there was never any thought of stopping people going. My sister-in-law went every weekend and took her knitting with her. All the mechanics would be coming and going and there was Muriel, Muskin as she was then, sitting passively knitting.'[4]

During the first part of 1916 the home defence pilots were gaining valuable night-flying experience and a marked decrease in the number of accidents revealed their new-found proficiency. On 31 January, when a large number of German Naval Zeppelins had successfully eluded British defences, of the 20 RFC and RNAS aeroplanes sent up to intercept the raiders, eight were damaged in landing accidents and two officers killed after crashing on take-off. Four months had elapsed since those tragic events and now British airmen were able to take off and land at night without serious mishap.

On 25 February the war struck the first of its many blows at the Robinson family. Grace's husband Arthur, a second lieutenant in the 8th Battalion of the Northamptonshire Regiment, died of wounds received in the Front Line and was buried at Lepugnoy's military cemetery. From his lodgings in Hornchurch, William wrote to console his grieving sister:

'My dearest G,

'I phoned Kitty up yesterday and told her I was coming over to see you today − But Stewart had arranged to go to town, so I'm awfully sorry I can't come. But Kitty tells me to come up on Saturday, so I'm going to her lodgings at 1.30 on that day.

'My darling girl I wish I had sufficient power of expression to comfort you in the minutest degree. He is a loss − a greater loss than I can express − to all who knew him, but my dear girl one is bound to gain some small consolation in knowing that one of the finest men on God's earth has met with the finest ends that man can possibly hope for.

'Your ever loving brother,

Billy.'[5]

An even worse tragedy was to follow, for in April came the dreadful news of Harold's death in Mesopotamia. Serving as a second lieutenant with the 103rd Mahrattas, attached to the 101st Grenadiers of the Indian Regiment, Harold had been taking part in the ill-starred effort to relieve General Townsend's beleaguered forces at Kut-el-Amara. The divisions attempting to break through the strongly-supported Turkish positions were thwarted at every turn and British casualties were heavy. Harold, struck by Turkish gunfire, was stretchered quickly out of the battle area, but on 10 April succumbed to his wounds.[6] To the entire family, especially William, Harold's death came as a terrible shock. He was only 22.

On the night of 25 April five German Army airships attempted a raid on London, but only one of them, *LZ97*, under the command of *Hauptmann* Erich Linnarz, came anywhere near the capital. *LZ97* dropped a number of bombs in Deal harbour, but was driven off by shellfire from Walmer, while *LZ88* only got as far inland as Canterbury via Whitstable. This Zeppelin, commanded by *Hauptmann* Falck, dropped nine incendiaries on Preston which fell in open fields. Thirteen bombs then detonated at Sarre and Chislet Marshes and another 15 failed to find any target at all. Falck finally went out over Minnis Bay at 01.35 hours. *Hauptmann* Wilhelm Schramm in *LZ93* bombed the Harwich area, but none of his bombs caused any casualties, although at least one incendiary fell between two training barrack dormitories.

Linnarz arrived over the River Blackwater at around 20.00 hours and headed straight for the capital, nearly 50 incendiaries falling in a line between Fyfield and Ongar, the Zeppelin captain confusing the River Roding for the Thames. At 23.08 hours he came under spirited fire from the Dog Kennel Hill gun and the improved defences came as an unwelcome surprise as a great many searchlights fingered the night sky:

'... They have lost us – strike, as it were, wildly past us, catch us once again, go on over us; one remains still, the others hunt around, crossing it or searching along it for the objective, while we steer in quite a different direction.

'The mad frolic continues for hours on end.

'We lose all idea of the passage of time as we fly on, every half minute releasing another bomb. Every explosion is observed, and its position pinpricked on the map ...'[7]

LZ97 now dropped a dozen high explosives on Barkingside, near Fairlop Railway Station, damaging seven houses belonging to the Great Eastern Railway, then nine bombs fell harmlessly in adjacent fields. The Zeppelin was next seen over Chadwell Heath, where it was caught in the beams of several more searchlights, and over Seven Kings railway station Linnarz was engaged by anti-aircraft gunners and home defence airmen of the RFC.

Of the eight pilots from No. 39 HDS aloft that night, only two fired on Linnarz and four of the others only observed the Zeppelin at long range and were unable to engage. At least one of the squadron's pilots was carrying the experimental Brock explosive bullets in his Lewis drums, Captain Arthur Travers (Ginger) Harris,[8] then B Flight commander of Suttons Farm:

'I have the honour to report that on the night of 25-26/4/16 I received the order to stand by from the War Office at 10.15. At 10.25 the first machine was ordered up. I left the ground at 10.30. Having orders to patrol at 5000 feet and east of the Aerodrome, I at once made my height, and turned eastwards. At 10.45-50 I noticed all the searchlights playing on a point north of Hainault Farm. I turned and climbed hard in that direction; at 7000 feet I could distinguish a Zeppelin at a great height, and in the beams of the searchlight. I continued climbing in a NE direction, as I thought the somewhat aimless movements of the aircraft indicated that it was uncertain of its whereabouts, and I expected it to turn east. My expectation was shortly realized, and as the aircraft turned I turned also, climbing and steering an easterly course. At 12,000 feet I turned back again and made towards the airship, which was then heading straight east and about 2000 feet above me.

'As she passed over me, I opened fire with my Lewis gun and Brock ammunition. The gun jammed almost immediately. I turned again and flew behind and about 1500 to 2000 feet below the Zeppelin, and managed to clear my gun, opening up again. A second jam occurred almost immediately; whilst freeing this jam, I sideslipped and lost sight of the Zeppelin, which had apparently at about the same moment evaded the searchlights. Shortly afterwards I caught a fleeting glimpse of it again without the searchlights on it, but lost it before I could open fire.

'Had I had a machine that would have climbed a little better, I feel certain I should have had a fair chance of success with the Ranken Darts, but I had the utmost difficulty in getting my machine up to 13,000 feet, the last 4500 taking a great time. I estimate the height of the Zeppelin when I first saw it, at 9500 and when I attacked it, at 15,000 feet. I was just over 13,000 feet when I lost sight of it.

'I distinctly saw signalling in and round London; the first I noticed being a white light giving five dots intermittently about four or five miles due south of Hainault flares. I noticed three giving the same type of signal on South bank of river somewhere – I estimated about Woolwich. At a point between Leyton and East and West Ham – where the Zeppelin was first caught by the searchlights – a very brilliant green light flashed intermittently for about 20 secs to half a minute. I noticed the Zeppelin immediately turned in the direction of this light, and steered a course over it, which would have taken it straight over Woolwich. Before reaching the river, however, it turned due east, and it was shortly after this that I attacked it. I have not the least doubt that these lights were signals; they could not possibly have been mistaken for anything else.

'I could at 10,000 feet plainly see the flares at Rochford, Joyce Green, Hainault and Croydon (?), the first three being visible at well under that height. Although I studied the Hainault flares particularly for some time, I entirely failed to eliminate an "L" of any sort from the display there, although I purposely flew over towards them on my way down at about 5000 feet, to see if it would be possible to see the "L" at that height.

'Lieuts. Robinson, Powell, and Stewart (the latter landed here from Hounslow) all report that the Hainault flare line, as used last night, was utterly useless. Indeed, both Lieut. Stewart and I had to study them for some considerable time before we were very certain that they were intended to delineate a landing ground at all.

'I landed at 12.50 pm. I have since found one bullet hole in my tailplane and three shrapnel holes.'[9]

Although he had left the ground later at 22.45 hours, William Leefe Robinson managed to attack LZ97 prior to B Flight's commander thanks to his BE2c having superior climbing qualities. At a height of 7000 feet Robinson spotted the airship at about the same time as Harris and climbing to within 2000 feet of it over near Barkingside he immediately opened fire:

'At about 11.20 (by the machine's watch which is some minutes fast) I distinctly saw a bright flash in the front part of the forward gondola of the Zeppelin – I thought it rather prolonged for the burst of a shell.

'I fired at the Zeppelin three times (each time almost immediately below it); the machine gun jammed five times, and I only got off about twenty rounds. When the Zeppelin made off in a ENE direction, I followed for some minutes, but lost sight of it.

'I saw no more of the Zeppelin, and landed at about 1.15. Five sets of flares were visible at my greatest height (11,000 feet), although Hainault Farm was badly laid out, there being far too many lights, and I could make out no distinct "L". The whole countryside, I thought, was very much more lighted up than it had been on previous raid occasions. The river could easily be traced from lights on its banks.

'I noticed signalling about five miles NE of Suttons Farm – it appeared to be five fast flashes, then a pause, followed by another five flashes.'[10]

Nearly all the No. 39 HDS pilots criticized the flarepath layout at Hainault Farm and many of them also reported the mysterious signalling that was going on almost simultaneously. Whoever or whatever was responsible for these 'signals' and whether any investigation was ever undertaken has not been recorded, but the supportive claims by the airmen could hardly have been ignored.

Linnarz made his way out over the coast accompanied by heavy anti-aircraft fire and eventually after an eventful flight of almost 12 hours made a safe landing, counting himself fortunate to have survived London's warm reception.

During the next day Major Higgins duly submitted his pilot's patrol reports to the 18th Wing headquarters in Albemarle Street:

'All the pilots agree that the acetylene flares at Hainault Farm are very confusing to land by. They also report that they saw extensive signalling to the Zeppelins from the ground.

'The direct line telephone to the War Office was hit by a Zeppelin bomb and cut. It is now repaired and in working order again.

'Hainault Farm reports that bombs were dropped by the Zeppelins all round their Aerodrome at a distance of one mile . . . '[11]

Along with Harris, Robinson had suffered the frustration of failure after his inconclusive attacks on *LZ97* and vowed that the next time he encountered one of the elusive night raiders it would be a case of, 'either the Zepp or I'.[12]

CHAPTER SIX

THE GIANT KILLER

The thing fell like the moon falling from Heaven, with a long trail of light — only the light was crimson, not green — and as it fell there broke out one of the most eerie sounds I have ever heard; hand-clapping and cheering from thousands of people all round, whose waking existence one had never suspected in the dark until that moment.

The Daily Sketch, 4 September, 1916

Saturday morning, 2 September, 1916, and Londoners, their night's sleep undisturbed by air raids, awoke to grey overcast skies and a light drizzle. The Zeppelins had stayed away for over a week and to many people the poor weather seemed to preclude a return visit that evening. Over a light breakfast 37-year-old city stockbroker George Francis Pinckard scanned his morning papers for the latest war news, although many pictorials were headlining Sir Douglas Haig's young daughters' participation in the annual juvenile angling competition on Deal pier, a welcome diversion from a world in turmoil. Beyond the front pages more serious reports centred around the Greek crisis as British and French warships arrived off Salonika amid growing rumours of King Constantine's abdication, while Russian and Rumanian troops had forced back Austrian units from Transylvania. On the Western Front 'Five Furious German Counter-Attacks' at High Wood were reported and three German aeroplanes were claimed brought down by British Front Line anti-aircraft guns. On the home front the Hon. Bertrand Russell had been served by police with a notice forbidding him to enter 'any prohibited area'; two railway employees, one an acting inspector, were run down and killed by a train at Birkdale; the Partridge season had opened to good shooting and *The Daily Mirror*'s gardening correspondent offered advice for autumn preparations, including the tidying of beds and borders, training climbers and maintaining lawns in good condition.

Of more pertinent interest to George Pinckard were the delightful distractions offered by London's many night-time 'amusements'. At the Alhambra, the popular George Robey was packing them in for *The Bing Boys Are Here*; at the Empire,

Leicester Square, the rival attraction was the great Drury Lane revue *Razzle-Dazzle!* starring Harry Tate and George Formby, while Alice Delysia, the stunning Parisienne actress and singer, was appearing in *Pell Mell* at the Ambassadors.

For those people for whom music halls held little interest, The Scala was running a number of official War Office films, including the highly controversial *Battle of the Somme* – few Londoners patronized such showings however; most families had already been touched by the war and now the Kaiser's airships were bringing it literally to the doorstep. To date the country's defence organization had enjoyed scant success and to a nation used to the immunity of being an 'island race' protected by one of the world's most powerful navies, the fact that German airships could bomb English towns and cities with impunity was a bitter pill to swallow. Pinckard and most of his fellow Londoners grew steadily resentful of the home defence forces, who seemed incapable of offering any effective opposition to the Zeppelin raiders.

Across the North Sea that morning the outlook for members of the German Army and Naval Airship Divisions was very different. After 39 bombing raids on England, virtually without loss, they were now preparing for the biggest airship raid yet mounted when, for the first time, both divisions embarked on a joint venture against the enemy. From noon of 2 September until 15.30 hours, a dozen navel airships arose from their respective North Sea bases: *L11, L12, L14* and *L16* from Hage; *L17, L22* and *L24* from Tondern; *L21, L23, L32* and *SL8* from Nordholz and *L31* from Ahlhorn. The Army contributed four vessels: *LZ90* from Mannheim, *LZ97* from Darmstadt, *LZ98* from Wildenhausen and *SL11* from Spich.

Weather conditions were poor over most of England and Europe. In London, it drizzled fitfully during the morning, there was a light westerly wind and a great deal of cloud. Towards evening, a light mist crept stealthily over the Wash and hung wraith-like over much of the capital and further up into the Norfolk Broads.

Well before the German airship fleet reached the English coastline, home defence units were at full alert. In Room 40 at the Admiralty, Admiral Hall's busy cryptographers and code-breakers had been poring over intercepted German radio transmissions for most of the afternoon. Things really began to hum around 17.00 hours, when the first indications were received that several airships had left their bases. Soon, the Director of Naval Intelligence confirmed that a large number of raiders were on the way and the defence organization began to swing into action.

Not far from Bacton, in Norfolk, Commander Alfred Rawlinson's Mobile Anti-Aircraft Brigade had dug themselves in; nearby was the coastguard hut where a telephone line was maintained to the Happisburg Lightship anchored some eight miles out to sea. It was an important link; airship captains made regular use of the lightship as a marker when steering for the English coast, so by ensuring constant communications, the earliest warning could be obtained of the airships' arrival. That night, Rawlinson logged the first bombs at 21.50 hours. Five loud reports were heard some ten miles south of Bacton and for the next half an hour or so, further explosions could be heard, along with the heavy throb of airship motors as the raiders made their way inland hidden from view by low cloud.

At 22.30 hours, Rawlinson made an entry in the log:

'Zeppelin overhead, crossing coast from NE, invisible in clouds. Altitude 5000 to 6000 feet; speed 35 to 45 miles per hour. Tried both searchlights; could not pierce clouds. Did not open fire. At 10.40 pm airship's engines went out of hearing towards SW.

'10.40 pm – switched off lights.'[1]

As more airships came in over his position, some were held briefly as the searchlights found momentary gaps in the cloud. Rawlinson took these fleeting chances to loose off a few rounds, but went unrewarded. He later recorded the feeling of:

'. . . "impotence" to which we were reduced when these Zeppelins hid in the clouds on passing the coast, although our beautiful guns lay within the range of their target, ready to fire, and our skilful gunners were "itching" to bring our murderous enemies down.'[2]

Barely half an hour after Rawlinson had switched off his searchlights, the officers of B Flight, No. 39 Home Defence Squadron were clustered around their battered, but treasured, gramophone enjoying selections from *The Bing Boys*. There had been no flying at Suttons Farm that day thanks to the rain, which had persisted for most of the morning and afternoon.

The atmosphere in the converted packing crate that served as the squadron flight office was fairly relaxed despite the fact that any minute could see a burst of frenzied activity as a result of news from headquarters. The scratchy sounds of the gramophone and the babble of conversation continued unabated for some while until the mess telephone rang shrilly and the orderly officer grabbed the receiver. There was a brief exchange as the word came through from Horse Guards Parade – 'Take Air Raid Action!' Then the hut was in uproar . . .

Tonight it was Robinson's turn to patrol between Hornchurch and Joyce Green, together with pilots from A and C Flights, who covered their own pre-selected areas. The airmen were to take off at one-minute intervals, Robinson to be followed by Lieutenant Ross from North Weald Bassett and Lieutenant Brandon from Hainault Farm.

Donning a heavy leather flying coat over his pyjamas, then gauntlets and fur-lined boots, his face liberally greased with whale oil to combat the cold night air, Robinson walked out to BE2c 2693, checking the Lewis gun, its drums filled with the new Brock and Pomeroy incendiary ammunition, before strapping himself into the tiny cockpit. The mist seemed to be closing in, but it would probably thin out at altitude, so there was little cause for concern as Robinson went through the standard starting procedure. When the engine sprang into life the ground crew, a man at each wing tip, steered the biplane on to the cinder strip already bordered by hastily-lit flares. The men holding on to the tail took the strain as the pilot opened up the throttle and the whole machine vibrated, then Robinson waved the mechanics away and the biplane bumped along the beam of the ground searchlights. By the time the third set of flares had been reached the BE's wheels were clear of the track. Then began the slow laborious climb to altitude as Robinson turned towards the Thames, where the flashes of many anti-aircraft shells were plainly visible.

All had not been going to plan for the German airship fleet. The keen wind blowing in from the south-west compelled several airships to turn back as ice began to form on their hulls, making them dangerously heavy. *L17* ploughed on up to Norfolk, but with several engine breakdowns to contend with, her commander, *Kapitänleutnant* Hermann Krauschaar, wisely decided to abandon the mission and headed back for his base at Tondern. Heavy rain squalls persuaded *LZ97*'s captain to terminate his flight and he turned for home when about 20 miles off the Naze.

Oberleutnant zur See der Reserve Ernst Lehmann, in command of *LZ38*, had crossed the coast over Dungeness at 24.00 hours and was welcomed by spirited gunfire from Dartford and Tilbury, leading the captain to assume he was over the London docks. Down tumbled *LZ98*'s bombs and, thus lightened, Lehmann's ship rose rapidly, steering north-east, where at 01.15 hours it was sighted by Robinson:

'I very slowly gained on it for about ten minutes – I judged it to be about 800 feet below me, and I sacrificed my speed in order to keep the height. It went behind some clouds, avoided the searchlights and I lost sight of it . . .'[3]

So Lehmann escaped and a frustrated Robinson, although by now exceeding his allotted patrol time, flew on towards the capital in the hope that searchlights might pinpoint another quarry. Meanwhile, other raiders were having other adventures. *LZ90* test-lowered its tiny *Spähkorb* at 23.00 hours, having shut down its motors, but the observation car broke free and fell to earth near Manningtree in Essex along with 500 feet of heavy cable. Since its bulky winch gear was now superfluous to their mission, the crew of *LZ90* pitched it out. Subsequent examination by British experts revealed hapless attempts by the Germans to arrest the car's progress, probably by jamming an iron bar into the gear teeth. Reports were confused as to whether the sub-cloud car was occupied, although no evidence had ever been found to suggest that it had.[4]

One of the airships arrived over the River Crouch at 10.40 hours, turning to make a wide circle so that London could be approached from the north. Passing over Chelmsford, then Colchester, the airship turned west over Saffron Walden and, attempting to get his bearings, its commander next steered across Royston, Hitchin and Luton before finally heading for the capital. The raider's subsequent course may be traced from Metropolitan Police air raid reports and statistics compiled in following days.

Between 01.20 and 01.50 hours

Six HE and incendiary bombs fell into fields near Bell Lane, London Colney, and St Albans Road, South Mimms. No damage and no casualties were reported.

Eight HE bombs struck market gardens at Bulls Cross, causing craters amongst lettuce and potato fields. The owner, Mr Hollington, was unharmed, although his home was narrowly missed by one of the missiles.

01.45 hours

One HE and four incendiary bombs fell at Enfield. One incendiary struck outbuildings at the Glasgow Stud Farm in Clayhill destroying one of the stables. Groom William Elliott and several stable lads saved five of the terrified animals, but three valuable race horses, owned by Sir Hedworth Meux, were burnt to death. A large amount of hay, straw and equipment went up in the fire, which took some time for the Enfield Fire Brigade to extinguish. No other casualties were reported.

02.00 hours

A bomb fell in Osbourne Road in Little Heath, Potters Bar, just outside Miss Bishop's house, 'Kerdistone'. The bomb, which made a 30-foot-diameter crater in the road, severed the water main; roofs of two adjacent houses were damaged by bomb fragments. Two incendiary bombs then struck a field in Bolton's Park, Little Heath. There were no casualties.

Between 02.05 and 02.20 hours

One unexploded bomb landed in the grounds of Eley's Explosive Works, Angel Road, Edmonton, followed by another in the Ballast Works, Angel Road, Edmonton. Then three bombs fell in the Sewage Farm, Montague Road, Edmonton. Neither damage nor casualties were reported.

02.12 hours

One bomb landed in the High Street, Ponders End; then another (near Southbury Road) followed by a third on Rochford's Nurseries, Durrant's Drive, Enfield Highway. The next three bombs fell in an allotment near Durrant's Park; Green Street, Enfield Highway (this one failed to explode); then Old Road. There were no casualties, but the road and a water main was badly damaged in Ponders End High Street, as were 63 houses, with various tram lines and telephone wires brought down.

Another HE bomb damaged several greenhouses belonging to Smith's Nurseries in Hertford Road, another fell on Rainer's Brickfield (causing no damage) and a third damaged three houses in Turkey Street. One HE and two incendiaries then fell harmlessly on Burnt Farm, Goffs Oak. No casualties were reported.

At 02.10 hours, having bombed Edmonton, the airship was directly over Alexandra Palace, where it was finally held in the beams of the Finsbury and Victoria Park searchlights. The Finsbury gunners put up such a heavy barrage, that the commander turned over Tottenham in an effort to avoid the dozens of shells bursting around his ship and as its bombs were falling at Goffs Oak three aeroplanes from No. 39 HDS, coming from the south-east, were closing in: Second Lieutenant J. I. Mackay in BE2c 2534 from North Weald Bassett; Second Lieutenant B. H. Hunt in BE2c 2727 from Hainault and Robinson in 2693.

Having failed to relocate *LZ98* amongst the clouds, Robinson soon spotted the second airship over the capital, its vast ochre-yellow hull illuminated by the nearby flashes of exploding shells. Despite the heavy barrage Robinson flew straight for his quarry, which was being violently manoeuvred in an effort to elude the searchlights. Momentarily it broke free and disappeared from view into a cloud bank – the gunfire ebbed. By now, thousands of people in London, and thousands more in the home counties, were awake and leaning out of windows, climbing on to roofs and gathering in the streets. They ignored the very real danger of bombs and shell shrapnel, so intent were they on the spectacle above. As the airship came into clear air once more, Robinson loosed off a red Very light and at the signal the gunfire ceased as the pilot commenced his attack. The BE dived below the airship's bow and passed along the length of its belly, Robinson pumping bullets into it from his upward-firing Lewis gun. The ammunition drum emptied rapidly, but there was no sign of fire, not even a spark. Clipping on the second drum, Robinson came in again, flying the length of his giant adversary with the same negative result as before. The airship flew on unscathed, its flanks glinting dully in the light of distant searchlights. It appears unlikely that its crew were even aware of the British aeroplane, for there was no retaliatory fire from any of the ship's gun positions.

Robinson only had one more chance, for the third drum of incendiary ammunition was his last. When he attacked the raider for the final time he tried another tactic, concentrating his fire on to one area beneath the hull. At first nothing happened, then a pale pink glow deep inside the vessel began to expand like a gigantic gas mantle being lit. In a matter of seconds the glow grew into an enormous ruby fireball as the entire tail assembly was engulfed. Blazing strips of fabric peeled away in scorched tatters as the doomed airship hung momentarily, its girders hissing and spitting in the heat. The whole sky seemed to be ablaze and the massive conflagration lit up the ground below for a radius of over 60 miles.

People at Reigate in Surrey, 35 miles away, saw the sky turn red, as did residents of Cambridge and the surrounding home counties. Most of the searchlights blinked out, their beams no longer necessary as there was a new and terrible light in the heavens. The doomed airship illuminated London's skyline with its awesome brilliance, 'like a great bar of iron fresh from the furnace'; to hundreds of thousands of people below, an image they would remember for the rest of their lives. It was the moment everyone had been waiting for and complete pandemonium broke out as people rushed out of their houses, singing and clapping; the cheering seemed to go on and on echoing over the rooftops. Many launched into 'God Save the King', and as children and women danced in the streets, railway engine whistles and factory hooters added to the cacophony of delirium. On the River Thames ships' sirens added to the tumult as the airship slid out of the sky, cremating its crew as it fell slowly earthwards. An acrid smell of burnt fabric and wood was reported to have remained in the air long after the wreck vanished from view.

One of *Flight's* correspondents, writing in the 7 September issue of that august aeronautical journal, offered his professional account of events:

'A little flicker of flame appeared at her nose, died down, and then burst into a bright light for about a fifth of her length. It lit the sky with a brilliant light that got more powerful as the flames ran along the envelope to the entire length. For a few moments I saw her full outline as a burning mass, during which time she continued to travel forward. Slowly, very slowly, she dipped her nose, forming a graceful curve, and then stood end up. This was when, as the flames roared up from the front and joined with those farther back, apparently opening the entire envelope and liberating huge quantities of gas, the brightest light was shown.

'Where I stood, ten miles away, it lit up the streets and woods until one could imagine it a glorious rosy sunset, for the flames were principally of a crimson colour. It is difficult to guess time under such circumstances, and watches unthought of with such a display in progress, but I should estimate the time from the moment she was hit until the final crash, which I distinctly heard, like unto plunging hot iron into water, as being three to four minutes.

'The slow speed at which she fell was amazing to me. I had expected, once she got nose down, to see her move at a terrific pace. But the mammoth appeared to be a huge mass of flame supported by a parachute. When yet some five thousand feet up, the light, especially at the lower end, turned to a brilliant ruby, lightening away through crimson and pink to an incandescent white at the top, the following flames, above, being pale yellow. Just at that moment there was a crackling as of exploding ammunition, or it might have been from the twisting of the girders, or the breaking of timber. Then she disappeared behind the trees with a crash and a final flare flashed up.'[5]

One of the scores of ecstatic residents at Homerton was six-year-old Harry Dobson, whose house was opposite the local police station. His father aided the police on raid nights by patrolling the streets and giving out warnings; often Harry would accompany him, much to the distress of his mother. When the airship had first appeared over London, a thrill of horror ran through the youngster:

'... It came at an angle across Wick Road on the edge of Hackney Marshes and pointing towards Leyton-Chingford, Enfield areas. My father was yelling at me to go indoors and I could hear my mother screaming at me to come in ...'[6]

As the anti-aircraft guns engaged the airship, Harry dashed indoors to shelter with his terrified mother and sisters huddling in the passage. The next thing they heard was the cheering, and ignoring his mother's anguished appeals the boy ran out on to the main road, which was illuminated by an eerie glow. He looked up in awe at the, 'great shape with flames pouring from the side'.[7]

Some 12 miles away at Suttons Farm, for those living close to the aerodrome, the atmosphere was electric:

'The orange light grew larger and spread forward. The significance dawned upon us. It was on fire. It was doomed. Finished.

'For a while the airship, still silhouetted in the searchlights, continued its course. The conflagration spread, the nose dipped, and it dived, blazing to earth ... I seem to recall the ends of the searchlight beams were tinged with a dirty red from the blaze before they went out.'[8]

To Robinson, the experience was almost beyond description:

'... I saw my machine as if in the firelight and sat half-dazed staring at the wonderful sight before me, not realizing to the least degree, the wonderful thing that had happened ...'[9]

Shaken and exhausted, he pulled his Very pistol from its leather satchet and loosed off all his remaining cartridge and parachute flares. To thousands below, these twinkling little red stars caused consternation, but those in the know, guessing their significance, quickly passed the word and renewed cheering rent the air.

The RFC had sent up ten pilots altogether, but, Robinson apart, their efforts went unrewarded. Only three squadrons were involved. Captain R. C. L. (Bobby) Holme of A Flight (No. 33 HDS) attempted a take-off from the Beverley aerodrome at 12.55 hours, but he crashed getting off and his aircraft, BE2c 2661, was wrecked, although Holme escaped unhurt.

The two pilots who had followed Robinson also failed to engage the enemy. Ross patrolled between his aerodrome and Hainault Farm for just under two hours, but saw no sign of the raiders. On his return to North Weald Bassett he made a forced landing and wrote off his aircraft, while Brandon, reaching a height of 9900 feet, returned to Hainault Farm after an uneventful 2½-hours. Engine failure compelled Freddie Sowrey to abandon his patrol 13 minutes after leaving Suttons Farm, when at a height of 2500 feet his engine cut out and he was obliged to return to the aerodrome.

Mackay had taken off at 01.08 hours from North Weald Bassett with instructions to patrol from the airfield to the river at Joyce Green, and at 8000 feet he headed towards exploding anti-aircraft shells. He saw nothing until he turned back for Joyce Green, when climbing steadily to 10,000 feet he observed an airship some way off held by the searchlights. For 25 minutes Mackay flew towards it and was less than a mile away when Robinson's bullets found their mark. As the ship was evidently doomed, Mackay headed back for Joyce Green, but before long saw another raider north-east of Hainault Farm. A 15-minute chase was terminated when the Zeppelin sheered off into cloud, and Mackay resumed his patrol for a while longer before landing at 04.10 hours.

Hunt left the ground at 01.22 hours to patrol the area from Joyce Green to South Farningham, and around 02.10 hours was at 10,000 feet, closing rapidly with the airship over the capital. He was 200 yards away when it exploded, and in the fire's glare he observed L16, which had just dropped bombs in Essendon, near Hatfield, some 1000 feet below. Although momentarily dazzled, he gave chase to the naval ship, but was forced to abandon the pursuit when Erich Sommerfeldt's Zeppelin vanished back into darkness as its blazing consort tumbled away. After vainly chasing another airship, Hunt returned to Hainault Farm, landing at 03.44 hours.

The three machines of B Flight, No. 50 HDS, left their airfield at Dover around 23.30 hours. Captain Woodhouse (BE2c 4588) patrolled for two hours between Dover and the North Foreland, finally reaching a height of 9000 feet. He saw nothing of the raiding airships and landed at Manston. Second Lieutenant Fraser patrolled the same area at a height of 6000 feet without incident, and returned to the aerodrome having been airborne for just under two hours, while Captain John Sowrey (BE2c 2711) met with similar problems as had his brother Frederick and, forced to break off the patrol due to engine failure, immediately returned to Dover.

To war-weary civilians who had lived helplessly under the threat of the bomb for so many months the dramatic destruction of a 'Zepp' caused great excitement especially among young children. One of them was 12-year-old William Clark:

'The "all-clear" was called that night; my mother told me to go up and tell my Gran it was alright to go to bed, and on the way up the stairs I looked out of a window on the second floor landing. There were distant dull sparks in the night sky. Looking a bit higher, I could see a Zeppelin. It appeared about three foot long – the "sparks" ceased, they must have been exploding shells.

'Now the Zeppelin was standing still. All was so very quiet as though all London was praying. Suddenly the Zeppelin changed to a massive flame which turned into a much smaller sausage-like flame rapidly falling head first to earth.'[10]

Youngsters who witnessed the drama in the sky above London would carry the memory vividly throughout their lives, the events of that September night as fresh today as they were over 70 years ago. For ten-year-old Charles Kirby, then living in Brickfield Cottages, Borehamwood, his most lasting impression was of the large apple tree in his parents' garden eerily illuminated by the glare of the doomed airship.

Over Tring *Oberleutnant zur See* Werner Peterson, commanding *L32*, witnessed the tragedy before turning about and making off eastwards, his remaining bombs being jettisoned over Ware. *L32*'s war diary, retrieved when the ship was shot down a few weeks later, recorded the awesome spectacle:

'A great fire which shone out with a reddish-yellow light and lit up the surroundings within a large radius and then fell to the ground slowly. We could see the conflagration on the ground up to the limit of the range of visibility.'[11]

Over to the south-west, *Oberleutnant zur See* Kurt Frankenberg's *L21* was above Hitchin. This ship never reached London either, owing to freshening winds, and bombed Norwich, dropping its entire load on Sandringham, having been fired upon by alert gunners there. Frankenberg had a long, eventful return flight to Nordholz, with engine and generator failures, the ship finally landing at the base having been in the air for over 21 hours. *Hauptmann* Kuno Manger, in *L14*, dropped most of his bombs on Haughley as he turned back via Bacton.

Strong headwinds were certainly a problem for many of the ships. *SL8* (*Kapitänleutnant* Guido Wolff) was turned back by them, his bombs scattered over Norfolk. *L11* sustained slight damage by shrapnel from well-aimed shells, its commander, *Korvettenkäpitan* Viktor Schutze, being able to observe other ships from a distance of 50 miles. *L11*'s war diary recorded an 'enormous flame over London, slowly sinking below cloud horizon, gradually diminishing'.[12]

The remaining airships had made abortive attempts to reach the city. In *L30*, *Kapitänleutnant* Horst von Buttlar flew as far as Lowestoft (although he later claimed to have reached London) and his bombs fell over the small village of Bungay before the airship turned back for the coast. Another who lost his bearings was *Kapitänleutnant* Robert Koch, who believed he had steered over Norwich and Great Yarmouth.

Attracted to the rows of flares at Bacton airfield, *L24*'s bombs fell harmlessly on nearby Mundesley.

Freezing conditions turned back *Kapitänleutnant* Wilhelm Ganzel in *L23*, and an engine failure caused *Kapitänleutnant* Martin Dietrich to abort his attack. Confused by conflicting radio bearings, he was convinced he had bombed the south bank of the River Humber, but with its hull beginning to ice up *L22* turned tail, crossing the coast at 23.20 hours. It was at this point that the Zeppelin was allegedly attacked by a home defence pilot, although no British fighters were in the area at the time.

L13 was blown north and bombed East Retford, nearly 30 miles from Nottingham, the intended target. Its commander, *Kapitänleutnant* Eduard Prolss, was attracted by railway lights and the ship's HE bombs struck a gasholder, causing a great deal of damage from the ensuing blaze.

So the biggest air raid on England, the first and only time that both Army and Navy Airship Divisions would make a combined assault, ended in failure. All the Germans had to show for 32 tons of bombs were the deaths of four civilians, the injury of 12 more and material damage worth over £21,000. On the other hand, they had lost a great deal; not just an experienced, highly-trained crew and over £93,000 worth of airship, but their morale had taken a sound beating, one that would never really be erased after that fateful night. For days afterwards, airshipmen were haunted by the awesome spectacle of falling dirigibles; it was but a portent of what was to come as greater tragedies followed in subsequent weeks.[13]

Robinson landed safely at Suttons Farm at 02.45 hours with little petrol and oil left in his machine's tanks. L. A. Aves lived just two miles from the aerodrome, and together with his pals had become 'friendly' with the crew manning one of the most powerful searchlights in Harrow Drive in Hornchurch. Young Aves witnessed the return of the victorious pilot:

'During a pause we heard an aeroplane engine. Looking up, we could see a solitary moving light approaching. Behind us the aerodrome lights went on and only then did we realize he was one of ours.

'Later the story went around that the aircraft landed with only half a pint of petrol left. Undoubtedly a "tall one", but after a long patrol Lt Robinson had little juice left. Before returning to bed one was conscious of sustained movement, a dull distant noise. Already bicycles, motorbikes, possibly a few cars, were on their way to view the wreckage.'[14]

Even before 2693 had rolled to a halt it was immediately surrounded as the station's personnel ran up from every direction and clamoured for details:

'I was greeted with "Was it you, Robin?", etc. "Yes, I've strafed the beggar this time," I said, whereupon the whole flight set up a yell and carried me out of my machine to the office, cheering like mad.'[15]

Fellow pilot P. Russell Mallinson later wrote:

'It was perhaps as well that his rapid descent from 10,000 feet had already done much to deafen Robinson, otherwise the ear-splitting yell that went up would have been a formidable strain on his eardrums. Also, it was fortunate that he had many lusty comrades ready to shoulder him to the flight office, for he was stiff with cold and cramp, and reaction setting in after the night's excitement added to his general fatigue.'[16]

Following a quick check of 2693 it was discovered that the petrol tank contained barely half a gallon; more alarming was the fact that Robinson had shot away part of the upperwing centre-section. The Lewis gun's protective guide bar had snapped off, the fabric was charred and the wooden ribs nicked with several bullet holes. But Robinson couldn't have cared less, all he wanted now was sleep.

As he was carried into the mess hut, the phone was already ringing. At the other end of the line was Lieutenant Colonel Holt from Adastral House offering hearty congratulations followed by a demand for a full written report. Despite exhaustion and constant interruptions, Robinson scribbled out his version of events before thankfully turning in for what remained of the night. Even as he slept the madness of 'Zepp Sunday' was beginning. From now on, life for William Leefe Robinson would never be quite the same again.

SL13, sister-ship to SL11 and virtually identical in all respects, is seen here berthed at Wildehausen in 1916. These ships were 'e' type vessels, of which ten were eventually built. Powered by four Maybach engines delivering a total of 960 hp, the ships could attain a top speed of over 60 mph. (G. BLASWEILER VIA D. H. ROBINSON)

The commander of SL13, Kapitänleutnant Pochhammer, leans out of the control gondola as the ground troop steady the vessel. Schütte Lanz airships may be easily distinguished from the more numerous Zeppelin designs by their forward engine and control cars being distinctly separate. (G. BLASWEILER VIA D. H. ROBINSON)

SL13 *prepares to land at Wittmundhaven − on 20 October, 1916 − note the forward handling lines already deployed from the two open bow hatches. For security reasons, ships' numbers were rarely applied to Army vessels, making identification difficult for latter-day researchers!* (G. BLASWEILER VIA D. H. ROBINSON)

The port amidships engine gondola of SL13 *with crew access ladder into the hull well in evidence. The large forward openings, which were not glazed, provided good all-round visibility and also doubled as defensive gun positions to repel aeroplane attack.* (G. BLASWEILER VIA D. H. ROBINSON)

It is the early morning of 3 September, 1916, and the remains of SL11 burn fiercely in a field at Cuffley near Enfield, Hertfordshire. St Andrews church (left) is correctly portrayed, indicating that this contemporary painting was more carefully researched than most others circulated at the time. (VIA S. G. ENGLISH)

Splendid study of SL13 making its first landing at Hannover on 19 October, 1916. Just visible along the top of the ship are the upper machine gun platform (nearest the bow) and the hoods which covered the tops of the gas shafts. (G. BLASWEILER VIA D. H. ROBINSON)

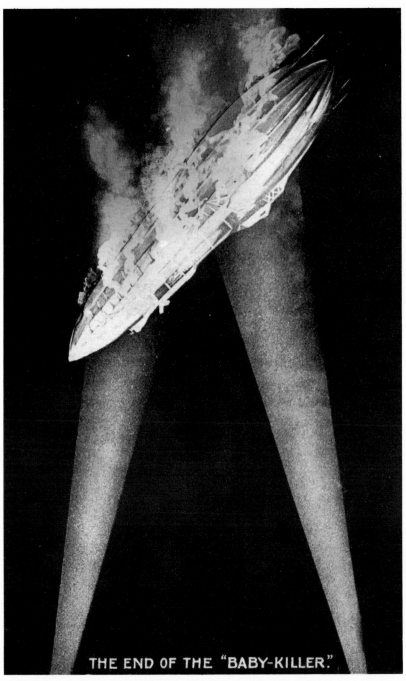

THE END OF THE "BABY-KILLER."

Scores of postcards celebrated the demise of the airship shot down over Cuffley by Lieutenant Robinson, RFC. Many of these were clever photographic fakes or just plain crude artists' impressions, such as this example. It made little difference, a delirious public bought them all by the thousand. (AUTHOR'S COLLECTION)

The Plough at Cuffley as it was in 1916, mere yards from where the blazing wreck of SL11 crashed to earth. After the war, the pub was rebuilt and in 1955 new gardens laid out on its grounds were named in memory of William Leefe Robinson. (CHESHUNT LIBRARY)

Not far from The Plough was the 'tin' mission hall church of St Andrews, which narrowly escaped destruction as the doomed airship fell close by. The building was turned into a temporary mortuary for the German crewmen prior to their controversial burial at nearby Potters Bar. (AUTHOR'S COLLECTION)

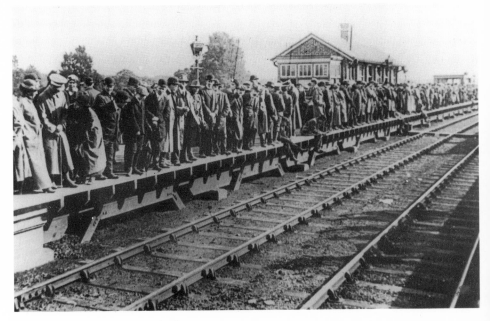

In the hours following the crash of SL11, crowds of sightseers made their way to Cuffley determined to see the remains of the wrecked airship for themselves. Thousands arrived by rail on specially-appointed trains — here, hundreds wait for one of the return trains to King's Cross. (R. WARNER)

The recovery of the 16-man airship crew at Cuffley was a grisly task and the badly burnt bodies were covered with a green tarpaulin while the coffins were being prepared. Despite the military guard, several visitors were unable to resist lifting the cover to examine the corpses. (P. AMESBURY)

Sunday afternoon at Cuffley, Royal Flying Corps personnel examine one of the airship's blackened Maybach engines deeply embedded in the earth. Apart from the engines, little substantial wreckage remained, the fire having all but completely consumed the Schütte Lanz's wooden framework. (R. WARNER)

Sightseers continued to arrive at Cuffley for days following 'Zepp Sunday' and the roads leading to the small Hertfordshire village were continually blocked by heavy traffic. Here, a stream of vehicles makes its way to the scene of the airship crash. (AUTHOR'S COLLECTION)

One of SL11's engine gondolas, with its smashed propeller, which straddled a hedgerow bordering the crash site. Although most of the wreckage was quickly gathered together and transported away, unofficial souveniring at Cuffley continued for weeks afterwards despite the risk of prosecution under Defence of the Realm regulations. (AUTHOR'S COLLECTION)

The biggest task for the military was the removal of literally miles of stranded wire cable, virtually all that remained of the airship's wooden-framed hull structure. Here, soldiers and policemen keep the large crowds at bay while recovery of the wreckage continues. (AVM SIR FREDERICK SOWREY)

An RFC truck piled high with wreckage prepares for departure. At right a large section of plywood girder may be noted alongside the tangled remains of one of the engine gondola frames. According to Intelligence records, SL11 carried not only Parabellum and Maxim Nordenfelt machine guns but also Army rifles for defence. (R. WARNER)

Scant pickings. Once the police and military had left, souvenir hunters were free to scavenge amongst the myriad small fragments of SL11 that remained. More than one enterprising local schoolboy earned a few shillings for selling 'Zepp relics' — some genuine, most not — to the many visitors to the scene. (R. WARNER)

A well-known photograph of William Leefe Robinson in BE2c 2693 at Suttons Farm. The airmen display the tattered centre-section of the aeroplane's upper wing damaged by Robinson's gun during his attack on SL11. The aeroplane's forward fuselage and wheel covers have been camouflaged with khaki dope. (AVM SIR FREDERICK SOWREY)

One for the squadron album. Lieutenants C. C. Durston, F. Sowrey, W. L. Robinson and Captain R. S. Stammers pose with 2693; part of the serial number is just visible on the aeroplane's fin. This particular BE2c was built by Ruston, Proctor and Co. Ltd., of Lincoln. (AVM SIR FREDERICK SOWREY)

Wednesday, 6 September, 1916. Inside St Andrews, Cuffley, sixteen Japanese ash coffins containing the remains of Hauptmann Wilhelm Schramm and the officers and crew of SL11 await the arrival of a Royal Flying Corps burial party. The crew were buried in one communal plot at Potters Bar. (R. WARNER)

The scene near the Mutton Lane cemetery at Potters Bar on 6 September. Crowds await the arrival of the funeral cortège from Cuffley. The military burial of the 'Baby Killers' was vigorously opposed by many people and extra police were on hand to prevent any possible trouble. (R. WARNER)

The RFC buries the crew of SL11, the cortège having arrived at Mutton Lane around 14.50 hours. At the cemetery gates a 40-year-old woman threw stale eggs at the procession, striking the coffin believed to be carrying the airship's commander. She was arrested and subsequently fined. (AVM Sir Frederick Sowrey)

The Reverend Hancock bows his head as the last few coffins are lowered into the large communal grave at the Mutton Lane cemetery, Potters Bar. After a brief service buglers of the Grenadier Guards sounded 'The Last Post' at 15.10 hours to close the ceremony. (AVM Sir Frederick Sowrey)

Following the destruction of SL11, pilots of No. 39 HDS accounted for two Zeppelins and the crew of one of them (L31) were interred at Potters Bar alongside Schramm and his comrades. This photograph shows the graves in the summer of 1937, SL11's dead being nearest the camera. (D. H. ROBINSON)

9 September, 1916. William Leefe Robinson leaves Windsor Castle following the investiture of his Victoria Cross at the hands of King George V. In a letter written to his parents some weeks later William recalled that the King was 'awfully nice' and, 'asked me all about you dear people . . .' (MRS R. G. LIBIN)

The chaotic scene outside Windsor Castle after Robinson's investiture, when he was mobbed by an appreciative crowd. It was some time before the modest young airman could be driven off to the comparative peace of the nearby White Hart hotel, where his sister Kitty was waiting. (AVM SIR FREDERICK SOWREY)

'Something untoward.' On 16 September, 1916, Robinson's night patrol came to a sudden and violent end when BE2c 2693 crashed into a hedgerow on take off, burst into flames, then exploded. Robinson was lucky to escape with his life; though shaken, he was unhurt. (AVM SIR FREDERICK SOWREY)

Very little remained of Robinson's BE2c after the crash which could so easily have ended in tragedy. As a fellow pilot later remarked, 'All that survived of the aeroplane that destroyed the Cuffley airship was a heap of smouldering wood, wire and fabric.'
(AVM Sir Frederick Sowrey)

The tail surfaces of Robinson's BE remained untouched by fire, leaving the serial number intact. Some doubt has been expressed hitherto as to the identity of the machine Robinson matched against SL11, but these photographs and contemporary accounts make it almost certain 2693 was the aeroplane he flew on that memorable night.
(AVM Sir Frederick Sowrey)

Among several items retrieved from the wreckage of Robinson's BE2c was the fin serial number, an engine connecting rod, part of the machine gun mounting, a section of strut and a Webley and Scott signal pistol which had its wooden stock burnt away. The latter was included in the Christie's auction in November 1988. (E. E. CARTER)

Typical of the souvenirs and mementoes produced in the wake of Robinson's victory was this matchbox cover. The adulation the airman was to receive was overwhelming: '. . . babies, flowers and hats have been named after me, also poems and prose have been dedicated to me – oh, it's too much!' (AUTHOR'S COLLECTION)

From the several thousand pounds 'prize money' Robinson received from a number of generous patrons, he allowed himself one luxury in the form of a Prince Henry Vauxhall. Seen here with Robinson are Lieutenant Frederick Sowrey and in the rear seat Captain Morton (nearest the camera) and Second Lieutenant Wulstan Tempest. (AVM SIR FREDERICK SOWREY)

CHAPTER SEVEN

DIE GEFALLENEN

In Memoriam
Hameln, 6 September, 1916

During a courageous but fatal attack against the enemy, my eldest, deeply beloved son, our good, true brother, brother-in-law, uncle and nephew, Captain and Airship Commander, Wilhelm Schramm, holder of the Iron Cross, 1st and 2nd class, met a hero's death.

On behalf of those left behind: Eva Schramm, née Hofmeister; Dr Otto Schramm, medical intern, at present at Alexisbad, Harz region; Maria Scheller, née Schramm; Franz Scheller, Captain and Company commander, at present at Braschaat near Antwerp.

We request no visits during our period of grief.

In 1916 the small Hertfordshire hamlet of Cuffley, near Enfield, was formed by a handful of neat, tiled cottages nestling in the curve of a long road that defined the crest of a sweeping hill crowned with poplars and tall pines. The contours of the village were that of a wide, clearly-determined triangle with the tiny corrugated metal church of St Andrew and McMullen's Plough Inn marking the 'base'; the cottage of Castle Farm at its 'apex' and two 'smooth, rich' meadows in between; a footpath crossing the meadows to unite the farm with the Plough. Directly in the centre of the triangle was a large barren field, its soil black and infertile, covered with tall grass, grey and parched. It was into this field that at about 02.20 hours on the morning of 3 September the blazing wreckage of a German airship smashed to earth in a shower of sparks shattering the tranquility of a quiet country village hitherto largely unaffected by war.

At Rose Cottage, a few hundred yards away, young A. K. Gogh, his father and the rest of the family had run out towards the railway station, their house lying near to the embankment. The Goghs had only moved into their home a week previously and could have easily missed it all:

'At first we did not dream it was the "Zepp" on fire, but some form of fire bomb as it got closer, for it was right above us. We could hear the crackling like burning wood, also a roaring noise as it was falling. We were so terrified we did not know which way to run.

'It did not seem very long in coming down, and just as we thought it was coming on us a gust of wind blew it across the fields to where it fell. There were very few houses in Cuffley at that time and within a short space of time, people began to flock out to see it.'[1]

At Castle Farm, seven-year-old Kathleen Holloway was transfixed by the spectacle:

'We were awfully afraid that the Zepp was going to fall upon us and kill us all. It was right up in the sky, a long, long way up, and was blazing all over . . . It was flying then quite straight. It then gradually came lower and lower, but kept straight.

'Then suddenly it wobbled, blazing all the time, and turned over sideways. A swift nose dive into the field was its end. I thought that we were all going to be killed. But I am glad to say that it plunged into the field between our house and the only other one near us, and did not damage our farm.'[2]

Sam Lambert, staying with the Shepherd family at Cuffley, was among the first to arrive on the scene:

'When we got over to the field we could still hear the crack, crack, crack of the cartridges exploding in the fire. This must have kept up for about twenty minutes. The thing I was thinking was that there wasn't much of a wreck there for an airship – only about twenty-five square yards of it. I had a great fear at the back of my mind that it might be one of our smaller airships, after all. Then we found the propeller. We saw four bodies burning in the wires – they were all black and charred, still burning. There's no doubt about it – not a man in that airship came down alive. There was a lot of burnt wood sticking in the ground everywhere around – everything had stuck in the ground end on. We even saw a broken Thermos flask.'[3]

Close behind Lambert came Special Constable Moore from Potters Bar, who was soon joined by Acting Sergeant Jesse White of the Metropolitan Police stationed at Cheshunt, some three miles away. At 03.00 hours, White, together with Constables Green and Leakey, discovered the gruesome remains of the airship crew:

'We saw three bodies near the propeller, they were burning and pinned down by wire. We threw some buckets of water over them and extricated the bodies. The first had his head towards the propeller, but his legs were burnt off and his arms to the elbows. The other two men were laying on their stomachs facing the other way. We got the three bodies to the hedge, the first was recognizable, the other two were not.'[4]

There were many personal effects strewn amongst the smouldering wreckage and on the most badly charred bodies there was hardly a particle of clothing left. One victim, however, was still clad in a fur-lined flying coat and had apparently jumped from the blazing airship. He was found in a standing position with his femurs thrust up through his body near to his collar bone. The remains of another crewman they found with a hand still clutching one of the control wheels and, assuming this to be the commander, the policemen laid it aside from the rest. Once all 16 bodies had been extricated they were brought together and covered with a tarpaulin away from curious eyes – for even before dawn thousands were already making their way to the crash site.

As far as the British public was concerned every German airship was a Zeppelin, but the raider that took two hours to burn out at Cuffley was of Schütte Lanz design. These were *wooden*-hulled ships, their delicate girders constructed from plywood rather than the aluminium used by Count Zeppelin's creations. It is a little-appreciated fact that the Schütte Lanz firm of Mannheim-Rheinau not only competed on equal terms with the Zeppelin company but also pioneered several improvements and refinements of rigid airship design and development.

The driving force behind the Schütte Lanz Company was one Professor Johann Schütte, a theoretical naval architect of Danzig's technical college, whose interest in airships was awakened by Count Zeppelin's *LZ4* and the subsequent disaster when the vessel crashed at Echterdingen. Following this he actually wrote a letter to the Count outlining certain improvements that could be incorporated into Zeppelin's designs. Recent research had revealed that Schütte, keenly aware of the growing 'Zeppelin-fever', was something of an egotist, tempted to share the limelight by building big rigid airships to his own designs and losing no time in seeking the means to transfer his ideas into reality. Fortune smiled upon the professor, who managed to secure financial support from wealthy Mannheim industrialist Dr Karl Lanz, and so it was that *Luftschiffbau Schütte Lanz* was formed on 22 April, 1909, with a working capital of 350,000 *Marks*. By the time *SL1* (largely designed by civil engineer Carl Huber) had been completed, over 2,000,000 *Marks* had been expended, but she finally flew on 17 October, 1911, and after a series of misfortunes was sold to the German Army for 550,000 *Marks*. She was subsequently lost on 16 July, 1913.[5]

As a result of *SL1*'s military success the German War Ministry, aware of the value of SL products as a national asset and as an 'antidote' to the Zeppelin monopoly, placed a contract for another vessel, *SL2*. In all respects this large rigid was a landmark, setting the pattern for all subsequent Schütte Lanz ships. Successful trials led to *SL2* being formally accepted in May 1914 and she flew to her new base at Liegnitz on the eastern German border, where she was housed in a special hangar. Further contracts were unforthcoming from the German War Ministry and the outbreak of war caught Schütte Lanz unprepared for the urgent, yet belated, request for five new ships.

March 1916 saw the first flight of a new design of Schütte Lanz ship. There were to be ten vessels in the 'e' class and *SL8*, destined for the Navy, was the first. *SL11* was also built at Leipzig in 1916. She measured 570 feet 10 inches overall, and boasted a diameter of over 65 feet, the enormous hull containing a hydrogen volume of 1,369,360 cubic feet in 19 gas cells. The ship was powered by four Maybach HSLu motors that delivered a combined 960 hp giving a speed of just under 60 mph. *SL11* made her maiden flight on 2 August.

Outwardly the SL and Zeppelin designs were markedly similar, but could be easily distinguished by their control gondolas. On the metal ships both control and first engine gondolas were immediately adjacent, on SL types, however, they were distinctly separate. Although favoured by the German War Ministry, the wooden-hulled Schütte Lanz ships were generally avoided by the Naval Airship Division, whose commander, Peter Strasser, certainly had little time for such vessels. In early naval service both *SL3* and *SL4* suffered an appalling number of structural failures, together with alarming collapse of fins and rudders as well as separation of glued joints, often in mid-air, which reflected badly on Schütte Lanz factory workmanship. This revealed the inherent weakness of wooden construction, which had other drawbacks, not the least of which was the lengthy building time such structures demanded. Through superior production discipline the *Luftschiffbau Zeppelin* could turn out 2,000,000-cubic-foot vessels in eight to ten weeks, while an SL design of equivalent volume could take up to nine *months*. As a result of these experiences, Strasser became strongly opposed to Schütte Lanz ships and scornfully referred to their champions as 'glue potters':

'The Schütte Lanz airships are not really combat-worthy . . . I consider it would be a mistake to build more Schütte Lanz ships, for experience has thoroughly demonstrated that wood is an unsuitable material for airship construction, because it weakens and breaks with even a moderate degree of humidity . . . Building more wooden ships would only increase the number of ships useless for combat and would create personnel problems for the crews of combat-worthy aluminium ships.'[6]

In reality of course it made little difference in combat conditions. When fired by incendiary bullets metal-built Zeppelins burned no less fiercely than their wooden-hulled contemporaries. But for the most part, mainly due to Strasser's insistence, Schütte Lanz ships operated with the Army and it was *SL11* that the German Army Airship Division turned over to one of their more experienced commanding officers and his well-tried crew in August 1916.

The commander, *Hauptmann* Wilhelm Emil Ludwig Schramm, was one of three children born to Otto Carl Schramm and Joseva née Hofmeister, whom he had married at Emden on 23 May, 1882. At the age of only 17, Otto went to London as a mechanic with von Siemens and within eight years had become director of the Siemens electrical combine. Wilhelm was born in London at 9 Victoria Road, Old Charlton, Kent, on 11 December, 1885, but five years later his father suffered a severe stroke and the family returned to Germany, making their home at Hameln, where Otto died in 1900.

As a result of his father's untimely death, young Wilhelm embarked upon a military career and in autumn 1905 entered the Second Eisenbahn (railway) regiment in the rank of officer cadet. He subsequently rose to the rank of *leutnant* and it was about this time that the national airship fever caught him firmly in its grip. 1910 saw *Leutnant* Schramm joining the Prussian Army Airship Battalion only a year after it received its first Zeppelin. In 1912, the Second Battalion was formed and when it moved to Königsberg, Schramm went with it, making a seven-hour, 341-mile flight from Tegel, near Berlin, to Königsberg in the Parseval non-rigid *PIII*. He was later promoted to *oberleutnant*, returning to Tegel as the battalion adjutant. Even before war was declared, Schramm had served in the Army Zeppelins *Z1* and *Z11* and subsequently as first officer of *SL2* under *Hauptmann* von Wobeser. It was in *SL2* that Schramm made his first raid over England on 7 September, 1915. This was one of the Army's more successful assaults and a great deal of damage was caused in the London Dock areas.

In December 1915 Schramm took over his first command, the old *ZX11*, and with this ship, and later *LZ39*, made a number of sorties over the Eastern Front sector. On 23 February, 1916, Schramm took command of the new *LZ93* at Potsdam and subsequently raided Dunkirk on 2 April; Fort Mardyck, near Gravelines on 24 April; and the next night attacked the Harwich area, albeit without success. Another attempt to raid England on 2 May was also unsuccessful as *LZ93* turned back due to engine trouble. In the following month, the Zeppelin was sent to Dresden for lengthening to improve performance, and after a short leave, Schramm and his crew was transferred to Leipzig and took over the new *SL11*. Following trouble-free trials, Schramm flew his command to its Western Front base at Spich, near Troisdorf, south of Cologne, on 12 August, ready for the autumn campaign against England planned jointly by Army and Naval Airship Divisions. An attempt on 31 August was aborted by bad weather and so the next raid was scheduled for 2 September, 1916. As *SL11* rose from its base on that fateful evening few could have foreseen the ironic tragedy that would occur several hours later when Wilhelm Schramm met his death just a few miles from his birthplace . . .

CHAPTER EIGHT

HAIL THE HERO

War Office
5 September, 1916

His Majesty the King has been graciously pleased to award the Victoria Cross to the undermentioned Officer:

Lieut. William Leefe Robinson, Worc. Regt. and R.F.C., *for most conspicuous bravery. He attacked an enemy airship under circumstances of great difficulty and danger, and sent it crashing to the ground as a flaming wreck.*

He had been in the air for more than two hours, and had previously attacked another airship during his flight.

The London Gazette, 5 September, 1916

J ust a few hours after he had collapsed exhausted on his bed, William Leefe Robinson, much against his wishes, was aroused to disgruntled consciousness by Freddie Sowrey, who unceremoniously bundled his friend into a waiting Crossley tender filled with officers for a 20-mile drive into the country. By the time the Suttons Farm contingent had arrived the Cuffley crash site was pure bedlam, the roads already choked with sightseers, forcing their driver to a standstill as thousands streamed to the little Hertfordshire village. The narrow road bordering the field was filled with cars, omnibuses, traps, donkey carts and farm waggons, and in the weak morning sun, the northern roads could be seen glimmering with the dimmed headlamps of hundreds of cars and bicycles. All forms of public transport had been besieged by scores of Londoners determined to make a pilgrimage to the spot.

A violent thunderstorm broke during the morning, and before long the field became a quagmire. Visitors may have been dampened, but their enthusiasm was not. As trains returned 1000 people to London, another 1000 came out to Cuffley. It was a scene that would be repeated continually for several days, but for all the efforts they made to get there, the public had little to see other than huge bundles of wire being rolled up and loaded on to waiting lorries. Burnt pieces of wood and cotton fabric were everywhere, and the smashed control car and four Maybach engines lay in various parts of the field: deeply embedded into the soft damp earth, the engines scorched black, and in the crankcase of one, a jagged hole plugged with cotton waste, which seemed to indicate that there had been time for quick shrapnel repairs before Robinson's fatal rounds had found their mark.

Despite a strong military cordon around the wreck, sneak souveniring continued unabated. At first the soldiers were tolerant, but they soon became impatient with the morbid curiosity of several visitors. When a man attempted to lift up a corner of the tarpaulin covering the crew, he was roughly kicked aside by a soldier, and a woman who had done the same, and promptly fainted, had a bucket of water thrown over her by one of the many RFC NCOs present.

Robinson's first visit to Cuffley during the morning caused furious excitement when his identity became known. Cheering loudly, the crowd surrounded him, and scores of smiling people fought for a handshake, whilst others waved scraps of paper, clamouring for autographs. Later on in the afternoon, he returned to the crash site, but with vivid memories of the earlier hysteria fresh in his mind, wisely donned civilian clothes, and almost immediately met a female acquaintance who ran up to congratulate him on his success. Robinson implored her not to give him away:

'I've already had one dose of popularity this morning and it very nearly killed me. My back's still black and blue with the thumps the crowd gave me. Won't you take me away and hide me somewhere?'[1]

Nevertheless many people who had cheered him earlier in the morning were still around and had little difficulty in picking out the young airman. Among many admiring onlookers was 15-year-old schoolboy Albert Hatt, who had managed to sell quite a few 'souvenirs' to eager visitors. The boy was especially impressed when several young girls threw flowers over the embarrassed Robinson.

Those visitors who had walked many miles that morning to reach Cuffley found themselves unable to get return trains in the evening. Resignedly they faced a long trudge to Barnet, over seven miles away, but by then many were utterly exhausted, especially young girls in light clothing for a 'summer afternoon's expedition', who had made no allowance for torrential rain.

Cars lay abandoned at the roadside by drivers who had miscalculated the distance and were now making heartfelt pleas for cans of petrol. It seemed that every available telephone in the district was besieged by desperate individuals phoning for taxis to come out from London and pick them up. The lunacy went on for days. In just 48 hours 10,000 people came by special trains that bore the magic word 'Cuffley' on the buffers. Indeed, so heavy was the rail traffic that King's Cross Station despatched two 'expert ticket collectors' to help out perplexed staff at the tiny Hertfordshire station.

Further scenes of despair occurred on Monday morning. Wearied travellers dragged their way home, whilst yet more arrived only to find the crash site a complete shambles. Only small insignificant fragments from the airship remained, which soldiers and police continued to gather. But newcomers had another shock. The Plough, the only inn, had its doors bolted and barred, with a curt note pinned up with the news that there was 'nothing to open with'. The landlord, Mr William, could have made a tidy sum out of extra drink and food, for even before breakfast the previous day the tavern had been completely cleaned out.

What was left of Schramm and his 15-man crew had been temporarily interred inside St Andrews church, which had itself narrowly avoided destruction when *SL11* crashed to earth a few yards away. The building became a natural target for the curious; young Dorothy Stead peered through the small keyhole of the chapel door and saw the 16 wooden coffins resting on their makeshift wooden stands. She was shocked by the sight of several policemen 'playing ball' with their helmets over the caskets.[2]

At 17.00 hours on Monday, 3 September a formal inquest was held for the dead Germans in the Plough's bar parlour conducted by Dr Lovell Drage, the South Hertfordshire coroner. Among several witnesses who provided first-hand accounts was a member of Robinson's own squadron, Captain René de Sarigny:

'We saw the burning wreckage of a Zeppelin [sic] in a field at the back of the Plough PH. Some police arrived and threw buckets of water on the flames. The commanding officer then went away and left me in charge of the wreckage. When it got sufficiently light, we picked out the bodies of the airmen, there were 16 and we covered them over. There were no identity discs on the bodies and there were no means of identification. There was a commander's coat with a badge and crown, but there was no name on it. Some personal articles were found among the debris . . . everything including the bodies was much burnt and charred . . .'[3]

Following Acting Police Sergeant Jesse White's account of his involvement in removal of the German dead, Dr Drage began his summing up by suggesting the airmen had lost their lives by, 'being attacked by soldiers using anti-aircraft guns.'[4]

At this the foreman of the jury interrupted, giving his opinion that an aeroplane had been responsible, which Drage countered by remarking on the lack of evidence to support such a claim. Then Captain Morton of No. 39 HDS addressed the 'court':

'There is no doubt about it − there was an interval of three to four minutes before the Zeppelin came down, when there were no guns fired.'[5]

'Then the gunfire had no effect?'[6] queried Drage. In response a jury member confirmed Morton's statement and the coroner, having acquainted himself with the new facts, asked if there were any objections to record that the airship was brought down by aeroplane. As none was forthcoming it was suggested that the name of the pilot responsible be mentioned. Further discussion between de Sarigny, Morton and Dr Drage centred around the manner in which the final verdict was to be phrased. The coroner added that there was little danger of the jury returning a verdict of murder − a remark which caused some wry amusement. The result was a rather naïve announcement:

'16 unknown German airmen were found dead in a wrecked German Zeppelin ship [sic] in a field near Plough Inn, Cuffley.

'The Zeppelin was brought down by the fire of a British aeroplane manned by a pilot, Lieutenant Robinson, Royal Flying Corps.

'The cause of their death was injuries, the result of the destruction of the Zeppelin, the same 16 Germans at the time of their death were male persons, airmen in the service of the German Government.'[7]

Having dealt with an enquiry, the next hurdle was to dispose of the bodies as quickly as possible. The War Office instructed the GHQ Home Forces to give the Germans a military funeral in accordance with the 'international code' and that the RFC were to handle all the necessary arrangements. The superintendent from Enfield's Metropolitan Police Division anticipated possible crowd trouble and arranged for over 370 officers to 'preserve order and prevent larcenies' amongst their other roadside duties.[8]

Wednesday, 6 September was the day of the burial, which took place at the Mutton Lane cemetery in Potters Bar, where one large communal grave had been dug for the crew and a separate one for the remains of the 'commander'.

Just before 14.00 hours a pair of War Department lorries, one towing a trailer, arrived at Cuffley and a few minutes later 20 members of the RFC entered St Andrews, whilst others lined the path from the gate. The coffins, of Japanese Ash, were then borne out and only one carried any form of identification, bearing a brass plate which read:

'An unknown German officer, killed while commanding Zeppelin L21 [sic]. 3rd Sept 1916.'[9]

This casket, in which lay the remains of what was thought to be the airship's captain, was placed on a separate tender and covered with a black pall as a measure of respect. A dozen coffins were placed on one lorry in two stacks of six and the others loaded on to its trailer. Thus laden, the cortège made its way to Potters Bar.

Although the funeral attracted a great many people, there was little sympathy for the German crew and the military funeral was not well received by the majority of civilians. Feelings ran high, the flames of discontent fanned by an inquest which had taken place at Essendon, just a few miles from Cuffley, the unlucky target for Erich Sommerfeldt's L16. When that Zeppelin's bombs were falling, two frightened sisters had run out of their cottage into the garden and were immediately cut down.

Their father, the village blacksmith, had been the first on the scene and found that both his daughters had suffered horrifying injuries. Shrapnel had killed 26-year-old Frances Mary Louis Bamford outright, and 12-year-old Eleanor Grace had received a dozen wounds on her left side, her leg so severely shattered that it had to be amputated. Despite the efforts of the local doctor, the unfortunate youngster succumbed to her injuries the next morning.

The funeral of the sisters took place the same day that SL11's crew were being lain to rest. The whole of Essendon turned out to pay last respects to the innocent victims, many people weeping openly as the four-wheeled trailers carried the flower-decked coffins through the entrance of St Mary the Virgin. The service had to be conducted in the western portion of the church, the chancel having been damaged by L16's bombs. It was scenes like this which so incensed public attitudes, there were protests over the funeral for the Germans and letters pages in local newspapers bore witness to the growing bitterness. The vicar of Potters Bar, the Reverend E. Preston, had been threatened with a riot and received many telegrams and letters from people protesting against the Christian burial of the 'Baby Killers'.

The cortège arrived at Mutton Lane around 14.50 hours, admission to the cemetery being restricted to servicemen and parishioners only. Several men bared their heads as the procession passed slowly by and many women, taking advantage of the warm weather, were wearing light summer dresses. Generally the crowds were silent.

The special constables and officers under Commander Gollin were spread throughout the route and especially around Mutton Lane, the south end of the Great North Road and the cemetery entrance, where most people had gathered. St John Ambulance men from Walthamstow were also in attendance, rendering first aid to at least eight onlookers suffering from slight accidents and fainting. After the coffins had been lowered into the graves the service commenced, the first conducted over the separate casket by the officiating Reverend Hancock, and Reverend Preston. The service was repeated over the remaining coffins and to close the proceedings, buglers of the Grenadier Guards sounded 'The Last Post' at 15.10 hours.

Only at the gates to the cemetery was there an incident. The spectacle of the coffins had been too much for 40-year-old Ellena Farrington. Hurling several eggs, one of which struck the 'commander's' coffin, staining the pall, she was promptly arrested by Police Sergeant 112 Thomas Ogden and on 13 September was brought before the Barnet Petty Sessions:

'Counsel addressing the Bench said the best answer to the charge was the fact that no breach of the peace occurred. The eggs were thrown and the crowd made no attempt to stop the lady. In fact the attitude of the crowd was one of sympathy. Mrs Farrington was the mother of three children. She was herself the victim of two of the Zeppelin raids last year. She was a witness of the two raids and upon one occasion was within 25 yards of where bombs burst. As a result of the raids she lay on a bed of sickness for some days and she was now a permanent sufferer from neuritis and but a wreck of her former self. Her children, before the attacks perfectly healthy, were now bundles of nerves . . .'[10]

The Bench retired to consider their verdict, having heard Mrs Farrington's testimony and that of her barrister, Mr J. D. Cassels, and Sergeant Ogden. Returning to the courtroom, the chairman, Sir Samuel Boulton, whilst sympathizing with Mrs Farrington's feelings, felt that a technical offence had been committed and fined her five shillings.

After the burial, the bitter controversies continued and the editorial column of *The Barnet Press* for 9 September was especially histrionic:

'So we buried with military honours the baked Huns brought down at Cuffley. Military honours for murderers and a Christian Burial service! What hypocrisy. Within seven miles from where we are writing . . . we have seen a village church and vicarage wrecked by Zeppelin bombs, cottages razed to the ground, amongst the ruins of which was found the body of a poor woman, while a girl, still living but with a leg torn off, was rescued in agony that ended in death. And the authors of such atrocities are given Christian burial and military honours! In such circumstances the Burial Service becomes a travesty and the "honours" are a reproach.'[11]

The following week, the paper carried a response from Sergeant H. Tinsley of the 43rd company RDC, who was among a minority who had taken exception to the editor's comments:

'They were not given full military honours, but it was an English and a Christian act that gave them part, and I fail to see how the "Christian burial service" can be termed "hypocrisy". Had we dug a hole in the field at Cuffley and put them in without coffins or a burial service, how much better should we have been or felt? Would it have stopped future raids, and should we have felt that we had done our duty as Englishmen? I think not . . .'[12]

Most newspapers, however, were more concerned with the youthful RFC airman responsible for the destruction of the airship. On 7 September, Lord French issued an official statement:

'Our experts hope to be able to reconstruct certain portions of the framework. The large amount of wood employed in the framework is startling and would seem to point to a shortage of aluminium in Germany.

'It is hoped that any persons who have picked up fragments of the wrecked airship will report them to General Headquarters, Home Forces, the Horse Guards, Whitehall, without delay. If of no value in the reconstruction of the airship they will be returned to their owners. It should be remembered that the retention of such articles constitutes a contravention of the Defence of the Realm Regulations, Section 35B.'[13]

The War Office and the Admiralty's Intelligence Division were quickly able to identify the wrecked airship at Cuffley, for at least three bodies, largely untouched by the flames, yielded a number of documents and effects from which much useful information had been gathered. The authorities were also familiar with the wooden construction of Schütte Lanz airships, yet to dampen national euphoria with pedantic technical descriptions was probably considered undesirable. Morale on the home front had soared and it was up to the War Office to maintain it for as long as possible. Lord French's communiqué was a masterpiece of propaganda and the night's victim was officially announced as L21, a genuine Zeppelin and one of several airships Room 40 had positively identified from intercepts of radio transmissions during the night of the raid.

The most well-known pilot in the country could not go unrecognized for long. Later on during 'Zepp Sunday' Lieutenant Colonel Holt attached a summary to Robinson's official account of the action:

'Herewith report by Lieutenant W. L. Robinson of his attack against the hostile airship this morning; a full "operations summary" will be forwarded as soon as the other reports have been received.

'Six pilots were sent up around London and others in Kent and Yorkshire. There were no casualties to pilots, two machines were wrecked. Operations were interfered with by fog in some districts.

'Lieutenant Robinson has done good night work against Zeppelins during previous raids. It is very important that the successful method of attack remains secret, and instructions have therefore been issued that the public are to be told that the attack was made by incendiary bombs from above.'[14]

The next day, Major-General W. Shaw, on Lord French's behalf, memoed Lieutenant-General Sir David Henderson, the RFC's commander:

'The Field Marshal Commanding-in-Chief has seen the attached reports, and will be glad to know if you have any recommendation to make with regard to any reward which you may consider the Officer concerned may be deserving of. He will be glad of a very early reply.'[15]

Henderson's reply was immediate:

'I recommend Lieut. W. L. Robinson for the Victoria Cross, for the most conspicuous gallantry displayed in this successful attack.'[16]

Evening newspapers on Tuesday, 5 September, had carried the headline: 'The Zepp-VC for Airman' and the widespread celebrations, which had hardly faded, swelled up again. The promulgation of the Victoria Cross, barely 48 hours after the action for which it was awarded, was one of the quickest bestowals in the medal's history and the press made the most of the story. It guaranteed the end of anonymity for William Leefe Robinson, who was showered with gifts, congratulatory letters and presentations which poured in from all over the country – indeed, at one stage the volume of mail arriving at Suttons Farm became so great that several officers were detailed to help answer it.

The modest 21-year-old became, literally, an overnight hero. He had grown into a young man of great charm; tall, slim and handsome. His hair was fair and wavy, his eyes a clear blue, and he possessed the kind of delicate features that epitomized the now almost legendary Edwardian blade, features that in following months would smile out from countless postcards, serviettes, matchbox lids, even biscuit tins. Babies, flowers and hats were named after him, bad prose and terribly contrived poetry dedicated to his victory; in some households his picture was in every room and at least five artists offered to paint his portrait for the Royal Academy. Robinson was to receive the kind of mass adulation familiar to film and pop stars of later generations – wherever he went, he was mobbed. As a result any chance of leading a normal life from now on was quite impossible and Robinson also found himself relieved of flying duties, being considered far too valuable a 'commodity' to risk in action. The authorities now had their home defence hero, who, in a single night, had virtually transformed the struggle in the air over Britain. Nevertheless, even they were unprepared for the extent of public reaction.

Robinson's investiture with the VC at Windsor Castle on Friday, 9 September, was an excuse for even more hysterical celebration, and during the early hours of the morning a large eager crowd gathered around the town's railway station awaiting the 12.43 train, which, it was rumoured, would be carrying the 'Hero of Cuffley'.

No fewer than six royal carriages, drawn by pairs of greys, were lined up waiting for a number of other officers due for decoration, but the vigil was in vain for, when the train finally arrived, there was no Robinson. Despite frantic enquiries, the mystery remained unsolved, and eventually the reception committee made their way out of the station. The six carriages had by this time already arrived at Windsor Castle, where King George V received and duly decorated those officers presented to him.

Meanwhile Robinson's sister Katherine, having previously arranged to meet her brother at the station, was also at a loss. It was not until 15.25 hours that Windsor was finally rewarded with Robinson's arrival at the stationmaster's house behind the wheel of a borrowed car, his own vehicle having suffered an untimely breakdown at Runnymede, three miles away.

The castle was quickly telephoned and the delay explained as Robinson, 'in a fearful fright', was driven to his destination. After lunch in the state dining room, Robinson was finally received by his Sovereign, and following the investiture the King plied the airman with several questions about the airship's destruction, then went on to discuss other topics, showing off some aerial photographs of the German lines. After quizzing Robinson about his family the King introduced him to the Queen, Princess Mary and Prince Albert, the Queen in particular expressing more than a little interest in the pilot's attack on 'L21'.

After this 'ordeal', Robinson had to face another. The crowds outside the castle surrounded the car in which he was being driven, shouting and yelling their gratitude. Eventually Robinson arrived at the White Hart Hotel, where he was met by Kitty and another large crowd, which cheered wildly as he was driven up:

'"God bless you – God take care of you sir," the people cried out. "More power to your elbow," roared a voice that might have come from a descendant of Windsor's Falstaff. "Take care of yourself," called out some of the people. "Don't be reckless," cried another in a fever of loving solicitude.

'There is not much chance of Lieutenant Robinson, VC, being reckless. His deprecatory "I only did my job" is the plain, self-made portrait of this modest, quiet hero, who has laughingly said that, short of a marriage ceremony, he cannot conceive of anything more unnerving to man than the congratulations of this week. His reputation among his men is solely that of an officer so keen on his "job" that he often works in the sheds with them like a mechanic. He is utterly sincere when he is abashed and nervous at the fame and glory that have come to him for only doing his "job". For the rest he is radiantly youthful and happy and ingenuous, a young hero with the pleasantest, most musical of voices. A wonderfully slim and lithe figure, a great and rather surprised gratitude to all who express their infinite gratitude to him – and part of this sketch of him is that when he issued from Windsor Castle he had hidden his Victoria Cross in its leather case in his pocket ...'[17]

Typical of the many hundreds of messages Robinson received at this time was a card from a young admirer:

'I salute you, and thank you very much for bringing that horrid Zepp down. I wish I were so brave and did so much good. I have 15 different buttons on my coat from my soldier friends also a RFC Badge which I shall now wear with more pleasure.

I am 8 years old, and send you my love and a big kiss of thanks. I shall be so delighted to receive a card from you.'[18]

While the Victoria Cross award met with universal approval amongst the civilian population, it was not readily accepted by a few fellow RFC officers. Such comments, though rarely voiced, often came through in correspondence:

'It is rather amusing to see that old Boelcke is taking to flying again. I should like to shoot him down, though I suppose one isn't much good if you don't get a Zepp down these days. Poor old Robinson must regret having performed at all. His life isn't worth living. All the risk that I can see he took was coming down again, though of course as a feat it was magnificent. I would rather attack one of those gas bags than a couple of fighting Huns any day . . .'[19]

Such jealousies, if that is what they were, may have been further fuelled by the huge amount of 'prize money' Robinson had received. Considerable cash awards had been on offer for some time, made by a number of notable and wealthy patriots for the first member of the forces to bring down an airship on English soil.

On 16 September Robinson was preparing for a night patrol in BE2c 2693 which nearly ended in disaster. Hornchurch resident Charles Perfect and a few colleagues were, 'waiting to witness the ascent, but instead, we suddenly saw a bright light in the aerodrome and concluded that something untoward had happened.'[20]

Robinson's machine had struck a low hedge just after leaving the ground, the tail had tipped up and the BE2c nosed into the ground, bursting into flames. Fortunately the pilot was uninjured and, clambering from the cockpit, he ran out of danger as quickly as possible:

'In the burning machine were a number of explosive darts, and Robinson's warning shouts kept officers and mechanics clear of the danger. In a few minutes the machine went up in one large explosion. All that survived of the aeroplane that destroyed the Cuffley airship was a heap of smouldering wood, wire and fabric.'[21]

The next morning some items were recovered from the charred remains of 2693, including Robinson's Scott and Webley Very pistol which had its wooden stock burned away.

Ten days after the accident which could so easily have claimed his life, Robinson was on a train bound for Newcastle upon Tyne for a special dinner at the Mansion House, the guest of honour of the Lord Mayor, Councillor George Lunn JP, who gave a lengthy toast to the young airman, after which he was presented with a £2000 cheque by Colonel Joseph Cowen. The Colonel, proprietor of the *Newcastle Daily Chronicle*, had, 'never dispensed money with so much goodwill'. Although suitably lavish the dinner was a private function, Robinson's superiors refusing permission for the event to be a grand public affair, for which he was 'very thankful'. The menu for the occasion included an *entremet* appropriately named 'Bombe à la Robinson'.

Robinson's other benefactors included Lord Michelham, senior partner of bankers Herbert Stern, who donated £1000; £500 was presented by Mr William Bow of Paisley shipbuilders and engineers Bow, McLachlin and Company; another £500 came from

L. A. Oldfield Esq, £100 each from Messrs G. Wigley and J. Ball and £50 from Messrs Jeremiah Rotherham and Co. of Shoreditch. Residents of Hornchurch presented the 'Zepp Strafer' with a silver cup for which almost 300 subscriptions were raised, and a gold watch was donated by members of the Overseas Club inscribed on behalf of the Imperial Aircraft Flotilla, while scores of other, smaller gifts were being received almost daily at Suttons Farm. The large financial awards were frowned upon in official circles and regulations were swiftly passed to prevent recurrence of similar gestures, much to the frustration of many patriots as well as friends and colleagues of some of those airmen who were soon to repeat Robinson's success.

Robinson sought to invest much of his 'reward' money with brother-in-law John Irwin's coffee estates, but he did make one substantial purchase in the form of a brand new car. The Prince Henry Vauxhall was probably the world's first true sports car and renowned for its extremely smooth running, a four-litre engine giving it a maximum speed of over 70 mph. Robinson's Vauxhall soon became a common sight around the roads of Hornchurch:

'Presently Captain Robinson's car came tearing up the lane filled with officers from the aerodrome, among them being the hero of the night, Lieutenant Frederick Sowrey. With him were Captain Stammers, Captain Bowers and Lieutenant C. C. Durston. They were on the way to visit the ruins of the burning Zeppelin at Billericay, and after receiving our heartiest congratulations, the car proceeded on its triumphant way . . .'[22]

Constant attention of well-wishers and admirers compelled Robinson to wear mufti whenever off duty and on at least one occasion the 'disguise' was effective. Travelling by train with his sister Kitty, he was handed a 'white feather' by an elderly female passenger, much to the young hero's amusement. Mostly, however, he was recognized wherever he went. When dining at a former favourite haunt, London's Piccadilly Grill, he now found it intolerable to be under the gaze of the other patrons and was quite unable to relax. Visits to music halls and theatres had similar results, Robinson unwillingly sharing the limelight with the stars of the show. The whole house rose and cheered him to the echo when he entered a box at the Gaiety one evening.

After the destruction of *SL11*, life at Suttons Farm proved anything but calm, and when Robinson's close companions Frederick Sowrey and Wulston Tempest shot down Zeppelins *L32* and *L31* on 24 September and 2 October respectively, the little aerodrome, always a popular venue with young 'flappers', now came under virtual siege by visitors, mostly adoring females:

'They had a lot of the actresses down from Town. There was Madge Saunders, and Heather Thatcher, an up-and-coming young actress; Leslie Henson was always down there; George Grossmith was a frequent visitor. Madge Saunders was at the time married to Leslie Henson and they used to go down a lot, but Madge used to "slip" her husband a few times and go down there on her own!'[23]

Among the more welcome visitors to the aerodrome was *Mademoiselle* Alice Delysia, whose talents won her many admirers at the *Folies Bergère* and the Moulin Rouge. She apparently had 'an absolute passion' for Robinson, although he seemed to have shown little serious interest in her or any of the other young women who turned up. Robinson's squadron colleague Sidney Stammers, however, had an eye for the girls, as his sister Vera recalled:

'(Billy) wasn't a man who went after women, he did *not* go after these actresses. My brother was the "rogue" of the place, there wasn't an actress in London that *he* didn't know. Alice Delysia fell very heavily for him and my sister-in-law would be knitting while they went off round the back of the sheds . . .'[24]

One reason why Robinson seemed to avoid the attention of so many female admirers was his growing romance with attractive Mrs Joan Whipple, daughter of Gerald Stapylton-Smith of Hutton in Essex. Joan was widowed on 24 November, 1914, following the death of her husband, Captain Herbert Connell Whipple of the Devonshire Regiment from wounds received on the Western Front. During 1916 she was working in a Surrey post office, but became a frequent visitor to Harrow Weald House near Stanmore, Middlesex, where lived close friend and confidante Violet Grinling. Both girls had formerly attended a finishing school at nearby Bentley Priory and struck up a strong friendship with another local girl, Nancie Vera Nicholson of Tile House in Harrow Weald. Sometime in 1916 Nancie became engaged to Captain Edward Noel Clifton of No. 33 HDS, whom Robinson knew well. Violet also exchanged lengthy correspondence with Freddie Sowrey, her letters full of frequent invitations for Suttons Farm pilots to join the girls for tennis games, tea parties and theatre trips. Violet's younger brother Jimmy, boarding at Harrow School, wrote often to Sowrey, this letter penned soon after Tempest sent Mathy's *L31* crashing to earth at Potters Bar:
'My dear old Bean,

'Thanks ever so much for your letter, it was sweet of you to write. Have you really and truly got the VC? Is it invested yet?

'How splendid that little beast Tempest getting the Zepp the other night – I saw it come down – Vi told me you were perfectly sweet the other day and took her to The Gaiety. I wish I had been there.

'Do you think there is any chance of your being able to get me a machine gun bullet or something from one of the Zepps? If so, do send me one . . .'[25]

For the remainder of 1916 there was to be no more flying duty for Robinson, and much against his wishes his time was taken up with a long string of official engagements. While an adoring public was hanging his portrait over their mantlepieces the War Office appeared undecided where to place Robinson himself, who pestered the authorities for a Front Line posting. A promotion eventually came through to flight commander and temporary captain, announced on 13 October and back-dated to 1 September, but there was still no news of any pending action. Several weeks later, on 7 December, Lieutenant Tryggve Gran, newly transferred to No. 39 HDS at North Weald, accompanied Lieutenant Colonel Holt on an official visit to Suttons Farm:

'. . . It was a rainy day and nobody expected an official visit in such weather. When the car drove up in front of the flying sheds nobody except the watch was to be seen anywhere. We walked over to the Flight office, where the sergeant was deeply submerged in a mass of papers. On our arrival he stood up to attention. "Who is on duty?" asked the Colonel. "Captain Robinson, sir," answered the sergeant. At the same moment the door was opened and in came the commanding officer of Suttons Farm. "One seems to take it rather easy here at Suttons Farm my dear Robinson," came in a sarcastic manner from Colonel Holt. "Sir," answered Robinson, "there was flying all night, and Lt Tempest has gone sick, and Lt Sowrey has been posted away." After this rather straight explanation the three of us made off for the Mess. The official attitude was very soon gone and before long Colonel Holt, Robinson and myself were sitting in front of a wonderful fire enjoying a good long drink. The conversation concerned flying, and especially it was the conditions in the north of England which were discussed. The zone of barrage from London to Edinburgh should still more be strengthened and it seemed that Colonel Holt wished Robinson to take command in the north. This idea, however, did not seem to fall in with the young Captain's taste. When the car, half an hour later on, passed the door with the Colonel [sic], Robinson exclaimed: "He thinks London is too jolly near my station, well I am going to volunteer for France at once." '[26]

It would not be until 9 February, 1917, that the long-awaited posting came through. Robinson's wish had at last been granted and he was to join No. 48 Squadron at Rendcombe equipped with the new Bristol F2A in training for operations overseas. While awaiting his posting, Robinson's engagement to Joan was announced, but if a marriage date was ever planned, history has not recorded it. None of William's letters to Joan appear to have survived, but he was to refer to her in a letter to his parents as 'the best girl on God's earth.'[27] No doubt he found in her a private haven of peace in an otherwise very public existence.

CHAPTER NINE

RETURN TO FRANCE

*... I attacked with four planes of my staffel. I personally
singled out the last machine, which I forced to land after a short
fight near Lewarde. The occupants burnt their machine.
It was a new type of plane which we had not known as yet:
it appears to be quick and rather handy. A powerful motor,
V-shaped, 12 cylinder; its name could not be recognized.*

*The D.III was both in speed and in ability to rise,
undoubtedly superior.*

*Of the enemy squad, which consisted of six planes, four were
forced to land on our side by my staffel...*

Combat report, Leutnant Manfred von Richthofen,

5 April, 1917

No. 48 Squadron was formed at Netheravon, Wiltshire, on 15 April, 1916, under the command of Major L. Parker, being equipped with the RAF BE12 'fighters' for service overseas. In June, No. 48 moved to a training camp at Rendcombe, Gloucestershire, and in February, 1917 became the first RFC Squadron to receive the Bristol F2A, of which much was expected. Perhaps gifted designer Frank Barnwell's greatest creation, the 'Biff' – as it generally became known to its wartime crews – was an aggressive-looking two-seat tractor biplane powered by a 190 hp Rolls-Royce engine which gave it a top speed of around 110 mph. Once its full potential had been realized, the Bristol Fighter proved to be one of the finest combat aeroplanes to emerge from the war and soldiered on in RAF service well into the 1930s. Its operational début, however, was nothing short of disastrous.

From the very beginning there had been a number of frustrating delays preventing the delivery of the first Bristols to Rendcombe. For one there was an acute shortage of skilled metal workers at the Brislington factory, as Captain G. Drydale of Adastral House in Whitehall reported on 29 November, 1916:

'. . . in my opinion two things are causing delay in the manufacture of these machines.

(1) Shortage of Tool fitters for metal work necessitating woodworkers being held up for metal work.

(2) There did not seem to be anybody at the erection works with enough authority to hasten the metal workers, and I would suggest that an Officer be stationed down there at once and told to spend his whole time going from the metal works to the erecting shop.

'New drawings have had to be made, necessitating several alterations. The manager of this Department promised the following deliveries of complete sets of metal fittings:

By December 2nd... ... ...   1 set

By December 9th ... ...   10 sets

'One item likely to cause delay is Duralium [sic] sheets from Vickers. They have promised to wire me if these do not arrive within the next day or so.

'. . . The B. & C. Co. would like Captain Jenkins to obtain permission from C.I.A. to build up the Shoots [sic], Ammunition Boxes, etc., on the machines by hand without first submitting drawings. They would like to be supplied with the first 6 machines. Also Captain Jenkins promised to write to B. & C. Co. confirming that they need not have any guns or Scarff rings on the first 6 machines.'[1]

Drydale concluded by summarizing the need for 12 more fitters with a promise by the Bristol Company that if such skilled personnel were forthcoming they would employ another 150 women in the metalwork shop. Drydale also noted that there were several problems concerning the armament, with no interrupter gear immediately available. Production trouble with the Constantinesco synchronizing mechanisms for the Vickers guns severely disrupted work schedules and on 16 January Drydale himself was on the receiving end of an enquiry from Captain J. M. Bentley, Deputy Assistant Director of Aircraft Equipment:

'In view of the fact that the subsequent machines are being delivered to Filton aerodrome minus interrupter gears, and that these machines are required for the equipment of 48 Squadron, can it be said please if any arrangements have been made to fit these machines with interrupter gear, and if not, when machines will be available so fitted?'[2]

Drydale responded:

'. . . From now onwards all machines will have the bracket and large gear wheel fitted at Brislington works and the interrupter gear will be fitted by the squadron when they are ready – the machines now at the aerodrome will have the bracket and gear wheel fitted there before going to the squadron.'[3]

Eventually extra labour at the Brislington factory eased production delays and with most of the armament problems overcome, the Bristols began to arrive at Rendcombe during February in preparation for operational service over the Western Front. No. 48 Squadron left for France the following month, under the command of Major A. V. 'Zulu' Bettington, arriving at Bellevue on 18 March to share their aerodrome with

No. 6 Squadron RNAS flying Nieuport fighters and No. 59 Squadron RFC (RE8s). Four days later, Major General Hugh Trenchard, commanding the RFC in the field, despatched a memo to the War Office:

'I would like to point out that No. 48 Squadron arrived out here with 18 machines intact all on the same day before noon.

'This is the first squadron to arrive out here like this and it was undoubtedly due to the excellent arrangements made and to the training of the squadron.'[4]

Having quickly settled into their new home the 16 officers and 83 other ranks that comprised No. 48 lost little time continuing their pre-operational training, although the pilots were forbidden to fly over enemy territory until the start of the big Allied land offensive planned for early April. As the squadron's pilots and observers familiarized themselves with their machines they were still experiencing teething troubles with the newly-issued Vickers and Lewis machine guns, most of which had been installed by their own fitters. One pilot who joined No. 48 in 1918 was Captain E. N. Griffith, who in later years recalled the situation:

'One of the early problems that was put to (Leefe) Robinson was the trouble the crews were having with the guns jamming up at height through, it was thought, the freezing up of the [lubricating] oil.

'The story we were told six or nine months later was that when the gunnery officer consulted (Leefe) Robinson as to what should be done, he replied that, "If the guns are freezing up through the freezing of the oil, stop oiling the guns and therefore there will be nothing to freeze."'[5]

During the evening of 4 April Major Bettington posted No. 48's first operational orders on the squadron's notice board. Three separate reconnaissance patrols were to be flown the following morning around the Douai area directly over the trenches from Bellevue. The day dawned shouded in mist, but just after 09.00 hours Flight Commander William Leefe Robinson, in F2A A3337, led a flight of six Bristols for the first patrol. Robinson's skill as a pilot was generally acknowledged, but he had no practical experience of flying on Front Line operations, having last flown in action over France as an observer during early 1915. Two years later the air war was very different as German *Jagdstaffeln* with their superior twin-gun Albatros fighters were exacting a heavy toll on many of the slower, obsolete British reconnaissance machines.

One of No. 48's most experienced officers in 1917 was Flight Commander Allen Machin Wilkinson. He confirmed that Robinson had been advised not to lead his flight over the lines at the low altitude of 4000 feet, nor adopt too tight a formation, which would prevent individual expression in case of combat. Wilkinson recalled that Robinson favoured a close formation for mutual protection; a common enough practice for corps reconnaissance squadrons at that time:

'. . . This method might have been successful if Robinson had been flying the FE2b and if they had not the misfortune to meet the aircraft of *Jagdstaffel* 11. Once Robinson's flight had been broken up, unless the Bristol had been used in an offensive role, which it wasn't, it could only be a matter of time before the experience of the German pilots overcame the group.

'Robinson did not appreciate the fact that the Bristol could be used as an offensive weapon by the pilot, and that it was not necessary to provide one another with protection. We were not bothered about Robinson's VC, only that he seemed to dislike any opinion other than his own in matters [of] which, I might say, he had no experience.'[6]

It may well be true that Robinson was unappreciative of the Bristol's 'dogfighting' qualities, but at the time so was almost everyone else and the well-tried defensive tactics which were so successful for BE and FE crews were initially, at least, adopted by the airmen of No. 48. Robinson's group also had the misfortune to encounter some of Germany's best fighter pilots as a *Kette* (sub-flight) of at least five Albatros D.III fighters led by *Leutnant* Manfred von Richthofen intercepted them over Douai just as the British aeroplanes were beginning to turn back on completion of their patrol. Selecting the rearmost F2A (A3340, crewed by Second Lieutenant A. N. Leckler and Lieutenant H. D. K. George) Richthofen's first, deadly accurate, burst had almost immediate effect:

'. . . In the course of an action my observer's gun failed him when an enemy machine was behind me. Before I could do anything my tanks were pierced and I received a wound to my head and in my leg.'[7]

Making a shaky landing at Lembras, Leckler managed to extricate his observer, who was mortally wounded, before setting fire to the Bristol with his Very pistol. Leckler's account of the action confirmed that at least some of the F2A crews were hampered by their troublesome armament. The problem was that some of the guns ceased to function not because of freezing but with little or no lubrication they appear to have seized up.

The 'Red Baron's' second victim was A3343, which he took a little longer to despatch. Lieutenant H. T. Adams managed to land the Bristol safely and, together with his wounded observer, Lieutenant D. Stewart, was successful in denying another new F2A to the enemy, nearby German infantry being unable to prevent the airmen from setting their wrecked machine ablaze.

By this time the remaining F2As were in trouble, being fiercely engaged by the rest of von Richthofen's flight. Robinson's formation had quickly broken up after the loss of Leckler and George and it was every man for himself. The flight commander and his observer, Second Lieutenant Edward Darien Warburton, engaged an Albatros, which promptly spun down – subsequently claimed by one F2A survivor as 'out of control' – before their guns failed them and they came under attack by *Vizefeldwebel* Sebastian Festner flying a blue-tailed Albatros D.III, 2023/16.[8] Despite spirited defensive flying on Robinson's part, A3337 received a deadly burst of fire into its engine and the flight commander's smoking machine was seen to spiral downwards. A fourth F2A (A3320) was attacked and shot down by *Leutnant* George Simon. Both Lieutenant H. A. Cooper and Second Lieutenant A. Boldison were slightly wounded as a result, but managed a safe landing behind the German lines and were swiftly captured.

Of the two surviving Bristols, one of them, crewed by Lieutenant Pike and Second Lieutenant H. B. Griffith, sent another Albatros spinning down 'out of control' then, having lost all contact with their remaining companion, flew back to Bellevue fighting off two more attacks and claiming another German scout 'driven down'. In reality, von Richthofen's *Kette* suffered no losses, although the Germans' violent manoeuvres in avoiding their opponents' fire could easily have been misinterpreted by the inexperienced F2A crews.

On 7 April Tryggve Gran was making preparations to ferry a night-flying machine from North Weald out to France in the company of Captain J. H. Mackay, who had taken Robinson's place as B Flight commander at Suttons Farm. The two pilots arrived at St Omer the following day and were having breakfast at a small café when a pilot who knew Mackay came over to their table:

'"Poor Robinson," he began. "Has something happened to him?" stuttered Mackay, his face growing purple. "Yes, poor boy," continued the new arrival, "Robinson took his flight in over Douai and was shot down on the way home. There seems to be little hope for him, because his machine was on fire."

'We learned more about Robinson's tragic fate late in the evening. An overwhelming number of enemy machines had taken his unit by surprise and almost exterminated it. Robinson had, according to what his own people told, fought with excellent energy and bravery. His machine guns had been seen to be in action until the last, and a number of machines had probably fallen to his bullets.

'When Mackay learned this, he seemed to get into a better mood, and said, almost delightedly, "Such a death is not to be mourned over . . ."'[9]

In the meantime Robinson's closest companion Freddie Sowrey, arranged for a message in German to be dropped over the lines during a routine bombing raid:

'To the Gentlemen German Flyers,

We wish to hear news of the fate of the Englishman:

Captain W. L. Robinson VC

who was shot down on Friday, 6 April.

We would be grateful to you if you could inform us in the usual way.

The English Flyers.'[10]

No immediate answer was forthcoming and early newspaper reports confirmed that the hero of Cuffley had been killed on active service.

CHAPTER TEN

'DISTINGUISHED SERVICES'

Major Baird replying to Mr Pemberton Billing, stated that the type of machine on which Captain Leefe Robinson VC was flying when he was shot down was a Bristol Fighter. Sir C. Hobhouse (Bristol E, L) — Is it a fact that this officer, who was reported killed, is now discovered to be alive, wounded, and a prisoner in German hands? Major Baird — I am sorry to say from the last news we had this morning before I came down to the House that we are not quite sure that he is alive. There is still reason to hope he may be, but it is by no means certain . . .

House of Commons, 25 April, 1917

For several weeks following his disappearance over the lines, Robinson's family and friends heard nothing to raise their hopes until Joan received a letter from her fiancée via the Red Cross. It was dated 5 April and William confirmed that he was unhurt having been captured following a successful forced landing near Douai. Along with the surviving members of his flight, including Warburton, who was also unwounded, Robinson had been taken to Karlsruhe, there to await transportation to a prisoner of war camp. From then on until the Armistice he suffered imprisonment in a succession of camps and the first was Freiburg-in-Breisgau; two months after his arrival William wrote a typically breezy letter to his parents:

'My darling Father and Mother,

'I have written two sheets to the best girl on God's earth — Joan — and have reserved this one sheet for you dear old people. I believe I have already written one letter or PC to you from this place Freiburg, at any rate if I haven't Joan will tell you all about it, and how I was transferred to this camp here from Karlsruhe with 19 other officers at the beginning of last month . . .[1]

'. . . are really very comfortable here and altogether a very cheery crew. I have two other officers in my room both of whom are receiving parcels, so we feed awfully well and start off with a regular English breakfast of porridge and bacon every morning – and sausages when we have them. I've got things going here a bit by now. We've formed a committee and I've started a library of English books (*Tauchitz* edition); we've already got just over 100 books. We are also getting up a sports club, and hope to get a club room out of the German authorities which we'll fit up as comfortably as we can. So you see life is quite pleasant here – although of course one gets awfully sick sometimes when you think that if things had gone a little differently we would still be on our side of the lines doing something useful instead of slacking here – out of it all as it were!

'I hope Jack has invested that £1500 by now – I wonder if he would keep room for the other £1500 till after the war, as it will be rather difficult to transfer the money from here. I would be grateful to him if he would!

'My fondest love to everyone.

'Ever your loving son,

Billy.'[2]

While he was reassuring his parents with talk of mouth-watering breakfasts and lending libraries Robinson was engaged in more important activities – planning to help dig an escape tunnel. Though he suffered from claustrophobia, Robinson, together with three companions, attempted to burrow under the prison walls. On 21 July he was writing to console his parents, having heard from Joan the terrible news that his beloved sister, Grace, had died in London after contracting malaria:

'. . . I can't tell you what a terrible shock it was – we understood each other so well – I might have done so much more for her. I might have been a far more dutiful brother. And what gives me such pain is thinking you dear ones will have to hear this so many miles from most of your children. How I wish I was with you and that I could try and bring you some comfort in my own poor way. But as I said to Joan such a loss as this makes me prize more, if possible, those who are still left to me. Joan comes first in one way, you two darlings come first in another. I firmly believe that sorrow does not come into our lives and go without leaving some good behind; this extra bond of love and sympathy may not be the only good this intense sorrow has left.

'After Arthur's death I believe the dear girl was never quite happy – but pray God she has perfect happiness now, and for that let us all be glad to sacrifice our own feelings.

'There is a devilish purpose in all things. How I love you dear ones at home. Mother darling you have still your baby boy – for I am always that, and will always love you dearly and do anything in the world for you.

'I am wonderfully well here at present and we have a very good time on the whole. We have formed a debating society and have arranged for debates to be held every Tuesday evening. We went to the swimming baths as usual yesterday morning and for a glorious walk afterwards. After climbing a hill we had a lovely view of Freiburg and the surrounding country – which is very beautiful about these parts. I must close now darlings – you know you have the deepest sympathy from your ever loving son.'[3]

During August the tunnelling was abandoned, but Robinson was as determined as ever to escape and teamed up with Second Lieutenant Arthur A. Baerlin of

No. 16 Squadron, who had been shot down on 28 April.[4] The two officers had been planning an escape for several days and each night awaited their chance. The guards uncovered the plot, however, and both Robinson and Baerlin were sentenced to be court-martialled for attempting to bribe the sergeant of the guard. It later transpired that Flipsen, a Swiss-German camp interpreter, had arranged to smuggle the two airmen out of camp with the help of more experienced escapees and for such services was to be paid a considerable sum of money.

On 14 September, a group of officers, Robinson among them, made an abortive escape attempt and the next night another was made, this time with other officers involved. Their plans were laid carefully. A small courtyard used by the sentries could be entered via a door in a corridor opposite the commandant's office, the path from the door leading to another in the outer wall and separated from the rest of the yard by a barbed wire fence. Robinson's scheme was brilliantly simple. It involved picking the two door locks and gaining access to the street beyond. It was of course impossible to cross between the doors unseen by the guards and so Robinson had craftily arranged for his orderly to hang washing on the barbed wire fence. Since the officers' orderlies had ready access daily to the yard, it was easy enough on the week before the escape for the amount of washing to be increased, making an effective screen. Robinson's orderly, a one-time locksmith, had agreed to pick the locks, but at the first attempt his nerves failed him. However, after much cajoling, he reluctantly agreed to try again the following night.

After roll call on 15 September the would-be escapers took their belongings into Robinson's room and at 21.30 hours donned civilian clothing, converted from orderlies' uniforms. Eventually Robinson and three companions, with Second Lieutenants Hamilton E. Hervey and Robert R. MacIntosh, were ready, but at the last moment Robinson's orderly let them down again.[5] The airmen pleaded with him without success until MacIntosh volunteered to accompany the man while he picked the locks:

'After about half an hour "Mac" returned fuming. Our orderly had successfully picked the lock of the passage door, but had absolutely refused to set foot outside it, and, to save further argument, had decamped to his own quarters. In spite of our disappointment, we could not but realize his position. If successful he had little enough to gain, whereas discovery would probably lead to a spell in the dreaded salt mines, a far worse punishment than would fall to our lot. There was nothing for it but to give up all idea of getting away that night, so once more we concealed our kit and went to bed, cursing our luck.'[6]

Within 24 hours another plan was made and no less daring. Hervey and MacIntosh were watching a German work party in the camp wood house when an idea struck them. If they could only get into the shed using the firewood as a screen, a hole could be dug through the wall and access gained to a known staircase that led to an attic from which windows would afford an exit. Alternatively, an entrance into the camp church could be effected and from there it would be easy to force open a window and for the airmen to gain their freedom. Within two days the plan was put into operation and, despite minor setbacks, the officers gained access to the church and at last managed to escape from a small window. Sliding down a rope, the airmen stole away in stockinged feet under the noses of the guards and made off into the night. Later, in company with Second Lieutenant C. M. Reece,[7] Robinson and Baerlin passed through a small town during their second night of freedom and it was there that they noticed posters announcing the break-out and giving full descriptions of the escapees. Later the weary trio came across an imposing hotel on the shores of a large lake, where, exhausted and ravenous, they hid in the shadow of the dining-room windows enviously watching the festivities taking place inside. They eventually arrived at the Swiss border, but within four miles of their objective, Stühlingen, an alert sentry challenged and recaptured them. On their return to Freiburg they were able to confirm just how heavily guarded that part of the border had been.

In time all of the escapers were recaptured and Hervey noted with some amusement how, even in Germany, the fame of Robinson VC was well known:

'Before being taken to our new quarters, we obtained permission to have a shave, haircut and general clean up. Accordingly, escorted by our guard, we repaired to the local barber's shop.

'The barber seemed very much interested in our adventures, and in the course of conversation asked which one of us was Robinson. This question gave us the first definite information that the latter has succeeded us out of the camp, and "Mac", for a joke, claimed ownership of the name.

'It was amusing to note the rapidity with which this false news was spread around, and every now and then a head bobbed round the saloon door to gaze with awe at the famous "Zeppelin Strafer". During my term of captivity, I did a fair amount of travelling about Germany with Robinson, and learnt that his name was as familiar to the German people as it was to those of his own country; wherever he went, the news of his coming preceded him, and, although he was regarded with awe rather than with anger, his fame was often most inconvenient. He was considered a desperate character and guarded accordingly.'[8]

After four escape attempts in as many months Robinson's reputation as a 'desperate character' was growing. In October came the expected court martial at Freiburg, the verdict of which had most likely been already decided upon even before the proceedings had begun and Baerlin and Robinson received three and one month's imprisonment respectively.[9] In the latter's case it was solitary confinement at the dreaded Zorndorf fortress, from which there was little chance of escape. The dark, dank cells were approached by underground passages and the only exit was a long, sloping tunnel which emerged in the centre of a large grass-covered mound ringed by barbed wire and a large number of searchlights. To the claustrophobic Robinson such confinement must have been unbearable.

On 2 May Robinson was to be transferred to yet another camp. This was at Clausthal in the Harz mountains, and together with MacIntosh and Hervey he was escorted to Kustrin's railway station. Locked together in the waiting room, MacIntosh told Hervey that he and Robinson intended to jump the train shortly after it left

Berlin and needed Hervey to share their compartment in case he could be of some help:

'Night had fallen when we boarded the train for Clausthal. Two compartments some distance apart had been reserved for our party – "Mac", Robinson, I and two sentries occupying one; the two dogs, Ortweiler and the remainder of our escort the other. As soon as we had left Berlin we settled down to a game of three-handed bridge, using a suitcase as our table. As we played we discussed the details of "Mac's" departure. He was particularly anxious to jump off before getting far from Berlin, as he intended to return there, procure civilian clothes, and travel by rail to the frontier. We were all wearing uniform, of course, but "Mac" had commissioned the Russian tailor at Zorndorf to line his military overcoat with a dark blue material, and this garment, turned inside out, made a passable civilian coat, which he hoped would be sufficient disguise until he reached Berlin.'[10]

MacIntosh took care to occupy a corner seat near one door, Robinson seated himself alongside with a sentry next to him while Hervey sat opposite with their other guard. It was obviously necessary for both Germans to be out of the way when the jump was attempted so the airmen had arranged that as soon as the train cleared the station Hervey would ask to be escorted to the lavatory. The suitcase which the prisoners were using as a card-table was to be left on the floor between MacIntosh and his guard. Once Hervey and his guard had departed, it was hoped that surprise and the strategically-placed suitcase to impede the guard's progress would be sufficient for one or both officers to get the door open and jump clear. The plan was put into execution just after the train was pulling out of a wayside station. Hervey and his unsuspecting guard were just halfway down the corridor when they heard a door slam and the shouts of the sentry. On their return to the compartment Hervey saw a dejected Robinson at the business end of a carbine:

'Everything had worked according to plan so far as "Mac" was concerned, and he had opened the door and jumped before the train had gathered much speed. The sentry had duly tripped over the suitcase in his efforts to stop him, but, being an agile youth, had turned and covered Robinson with his rifle in time to prevent him from reaching the opposite door. Meanwhile, the second sentry, returning and seeing what had happened, pulled the emergency cord and stopped the train. For a few minutes pandemonium reigned. Whistles blew, heads were thrust excitedly out of carriage windows, while the guard and a few soldiers and civilians dashed down the line in pursuit of "Mac". After a brief and fruitless search in the darkness they returned, our train steamed slowly back into the station, and we were all bundled out and securely locked up in the waiting room.'[11]

Arriving at Clausthal, Robinson found himself under the jurisdiction of one of the notorious Niemeyer twins. Heinrich and Karl were commandants of the Clausthal and Holzminden POW camps respectively and their harsh treatment of Allied prisoners has been well documented. The brothers had spent several years in the USA prior to the war, where they had picked up some English and a good deal of American bar-room slang.

Their animated tirades directed at their charges, during which they would go red in the face and utter preposterous threats in their fractured Anglo-American, would have been laughable in less serious circumstances. Karl's most priceless gem was widely appreciated by the prisoners: 'You think I do not understand the English, but I do. I know damn all about you!'[12]

Heinrich, known to most Allied prisoners who came under his jurisdiction as 'Milwaukee Bill', took an instant dislike to Robinson although, initially, life for the VC airman was tolerable enough and he was not denied any of the usual privileges the Geneva convention accorded to an officer POW. His pass card, which survives, reveals that he was allowed a certain measure of freedom. In view of his many escape attempts for which he was subsequently mentioned in despatches, the wording of the card is somewhat ironic:

'By this card I give my word of honour that during the walks outside the camp, I will not escape nor attempt to make an escape, nor will I make any preparations to do so, nor will I attempt to commit any action during this time to the prejudice of the German Empire. I give hereby my word of honour to use this card only myself and not give it to any other prisoner of war.'[13]

The various Red Cross parcels and letters from family and well-wishers that Robinson received did much to keep up his morale. Typical of the mail he received was this from a little girl who, in 1918, still fondly remembered the 'Cuffley VC':

'Dear Captain Robinson,

'I have been knitting a woollen scarf, and I want you to have it, as you are the first VC airman of this war, in England. My mother wrote to Captain Sowrey to find out your address, I daresay you remember that about a year ago, mother sent you your photograph to autograph. We have it in our dining-room, framed, with a Union Jack over it. I have got two photographs of you in my bedroom, and in every other room in the house there is one.

'I do hope you will get the parcel alright, as I do not want someone, whom I don't know, or of whom I have never heard, to have it, as I have taken a great deal of trouble over the scarf.

'With kindest regards, I remain

Yours very sincerely

Annie C. Rogers.'[14]

During July Robinson was transferred to Holzminden by Niemeyer, who handed him over to his brother Karl. The Clausthal camp commandant who had taken an aversion to the airman from the day he arrived was quick to be rid of him.

In conversation with the author in early 1989, Squadron Leader Hervey recalled his experiences of Clausthal. He remembered Robinson as a modest man whose powerful voice made him popular at camp concerts and he had recollections of the furore caused within the Robinson family when Alice Delysia on receipt of a letter to her from William had it published in the newspapers! Robinson would later confide to Hervey that his engagement had been 'hurried' and that he was 'having second thoughts' about marriage.

He also confirmed that during the skirmish over Douai when he was brought down, his guns were not operating properly. When Robinson left for Holzminden, Hervey much regretted his departure – he never saw him again.

Under Karl Niemeyer Robinson suffered ceaseless and deliberate persecution and got off to a bad start by almost immediately escaping along with Captain W. S. Stephenson of No. 73 Squadron.[15] They were soon recaptured, however, and each thrown into solitary confinement. Niemeyer hated escapers, viewing their activities as personal affronts aimed at undermining his authority. When Robinson was recaptured Niemeyer raged at him in his almost comic English and, it is alleged, swore to avenge the death of Wilhelm Schramm, whom he falsely claimed to have known well, going out of his way to make life difficult for Robinson, whose fellow prisoners were incensed at the treatment he received:

'The Boche harried and badgered and bullied him in every way possible. He wasn't in any way physically ill-treated, but they were always having special roll calls for him, waking him up at night to see if he was still there, etc. All this must have bothered him a great deal.'[16]

The British adjutant at Holzminden was H. F. G. Durnford of the RFA, and he provided further evidence of Robinson's persecution. Officers suspected of being involved in escape preparations soon found themselves bundled unceremoniously into the ground floor cells of 'A' *Kaserne*:

'. . . where the lower windows were never open and the flies and staleness of the atmosphere were correspondingly oppressive. Billets in this way were found for any officers who had been known to have escaped before and who were referred to feelingly by Niemeyer as "the yentlemen". These particular rooms used to be visited two or three times in a night by a *feldwebel* with an electric torch, which he used to flash on the occupant of each bed in turn, thereby effectually waking everybody up. Here lay the aforementioned and eloquent Beyfus, whose recent arrival had prevented his obtaining a place in the tunnel scheme, but whose record made him a marked man with the authorities. Here I myself lay, after yet another enforced migration from the attic floor in A House, and in accordance – so lied the official intimation – with orders from Hanover. And here also lay Leefe Robinson VC, whose gallant spirit Niemeyer, with subtle cruelty, had endeavoured for months past to break . . .

'. . . The handling to which Leefe Robinson was subjected was so outrageous that it was communicated to the home authorities in a concealed report (in the hollow of a tennis racket handle) via an exchange party. Robinson had come from Freiburg in Baden, where he had made an attempt with several others to escape. "The English Richthofen" – as Niemeyer, with coarse urbanity, called him to his face – was at once singled out as the victim of a malevolent scheme of repression. He was placed in the most uncomfortable room in the camp, whereas his rank entitled him to the privilege of a small room; he was caused to answer to a special *appel* two or three times in a day; and he was forbidden under any pretext to enter *Kaserne* B.

'On the occasion of a visit from some inspecting general, and on the pretext of all the rooms having to be cleaned up and ready for inspection by 9 o'clock *appel*, Robinson's room was entered by a *feldwebel* and sentries at 7.45 and Robinson himself was forcibly pulled out of bed and the table next to the bed upset on the floor. Two hours later, Niemeyer was introducing "the English Richthofen" to the august visitor with a profusion of oleaginous compliments, and four hours later Robinson was in the cells for having disobeyed camp orders.'[17]

In his memoirs, published in 1919, Tryggve Gran recalled another incident:

'One of Robinson's guards, by his cruel acts, tried to make his time in the camp a living hell on earth. His methods were numerous and in 1918, when the ration of food was so small that they were almost starving, employed a devilish strategy. Captain Robinson ate in a separate room. One day as he arrived at the usual time for dinner, he found written on the door, *Eintreten verboten!* Robinson didn't care about this, went in and ate his ordinary meal. Some time after the camp commandant arrived with a number of sentries, Robinson was taken to a cell and, for disobeying an "order", was whipped to the point of collapse.'[18]

Not surprisingly such experiences took their toll on Robinson and when the Armistice was signed in November 1918, he was not in the best of health. For a few days prior to boarding the ship back to England Robinson stayed in Denmark. During the war that country was not the industrial one it is nowadays and in those agricultural times suffered no lack of food. Danish citizens learned that Allied officers had a hard time in the camps, and were asked by the Red Cross to contribute gift parcels. One citizen, the notable pre-war pilot Erik Hildesheim, specified that the recipient of his parcels should be an airman. In due course he received a grateful letter from Robinson, who when repatriated via Denmark, received an invitation from his benefactor. The 'committee in charge of arrangements' would not permit this, and Robinson was booked into the Terminus Hotel opposite Copenhagen's main railway station. Nevertheless, Hildesheim stood him a dinner:

'He was not much for wet wares, but enjoyed the rich Danish food and particularly succumbed to whipped cream. I told him that I did not begrudge him any amount he could enjoy and stand. However, I warned him that he had better go a bit easy after the lean diet that his stomach had to endure for so long.

'It was a very sick Leefe Robinson and a sad sight I met when calling for him the next morning to take him for the sights of the town. He was in bed and groaning, his head swollen, and his skin very red. I quickly called a doctor and for the rest of his four-day stay in Copenhagen, poor Leefe was permitted to consume nothing but water wherein potatoes had been boiled.'[19]

Having recovered from the dramatic after-effects of his Danish friend's hospitality Robinson at last boarded one of the POW repatriation ships bound for England – he was going home.

CHAPTER ELEVEN

'LIFE'S RACE WELL RUN'

Captain W. Leefe Robinson VC, who brought down the first Zeppelin in England, was buried in the village cemetery of Harrow Weald on Friday afternoon. There had been a suggestion that the famous airman should be interred at Cuffley, the scene of his great exploit on 3 September, 1916. The obsequies at Harrow Weald, where he lies by desire of his dearest friends, were of the simplest character; but not more simple than was in accord with the modest, reserved, and boyish character of the youthful winner of the highest award for valour.

The Harrow Observer, 10 January, 1919

Robinson's ship dropped anchor at the port of Leith near Edinburgh on 14 December, 1918. In the company of hundreds of other ex-prisoners he was sent to the POW reception camp at Ripon in North Yorkshire, where, following an interview with the commanding officer, Captain O. W. Caye, he was granted an ordinary leave valid up to 15 February, 1919, the certificate which Robinson pocketed entitling him to food cards which would be provided by the local Food Controller on presentation of the document. Robinson's long-term future was by no means certain. In earlier, happier, years there had been serious talk of managing Harold's tea plantation in Coimbature, but his brother's death in Mesopotamia had shattered that dream; what Robinson's intentions were at this point in his life remain conjecture.

The first Christmas of peace for four years was an excuse for real celebration and after a brief visit to Suttons Farm to see his old comrades there, Robinson travelled to Harrow Weald on 23 December to spend the festive season with Nancie and Edward Clifton at their Lavender Cottage in Gordon Avenue, where he was reunited with Joan and his sister Katherine. Several people who remembered his return recalled that his back was 'bent over' and that he needed the support of a walking stick, but at least he was surrounded by loving friends, which doubtless did a great deal to raise his spirits.[1] What occurred just a few days later was the cruellest irony, for Robinson contracted the deadly influenza virus and the Cliftons, deeply concerned over his worsening condition, confined him to bed. At that time the entire world was in the tight grip of an influenza pandemic, a second wave of a milder epidemic that had occurred in the middle of 1918. This time, however, it was very different, the strain was far more deadly and spread with terrifying rapidity. Symptoms varied, but it usually began in a mild way, coughing and sneezing, then pulmonary complications might set in after the passage of a few hours. The hapless patient then suffered severe infective inflammation which could develop variously into bronchial pneumonia with virulent toxaemic, or even septicaemic, blood poisoning. After 24 hours such complications could prove fatal.

Perhaps the most surprising aspect of the catastrophe was the high number of potentially *healthy* young victims. Broadly speaking, over the 1918-19 period worldwide, 45 per cent of those who died were in the 15-35 age group. The final total of deaths is a conservative one, *27,000,000* is one figure advanced by several historians. It was in India that the worst figures were estimated; in that sorry country more people died as a result of the disease than were killed during the entire war. In England some 150,000 died and the pandemic was no respecter of persons; it nearly claimed the life of David Lloyd George, the British Prime Minister, who was stricken after the Armistice and kept in bed for ten days in Manchester's Town Hall. The 'Welsh Wizard' was lucky, he survived – William Leefe Robinson would not be so fortunate. The end came suddenly, the 'Zepp Strafer' succumbing on Tuesday, 31 December with Joan and the Cliftons at his bedside during the last moments. The local coroner subsequently recorded a verdict of 'Cardiac Failure brought on by influenza'.[2] The victim was just 23 years old.

Local gossip hinted that the late captain's relatives blamed Joan for the tragedy, suggesting that by 'showing him off' to all her friends in the district made him more susceptible to infection. Considering the disease was at its peak during December and so widespread, such an accusation, if true, was hardly legitimate. Much has been made of Robinson's poor health on his return to England, the blame being laid at the feet of Camp Commandant Niemeyer, whose ill-treatment of the airman is a matter of record:

'Baroness Heyking[3] and Mrs Whipple have asked the Government to arrest Niemeyer and bring him to immediate justice. The bully deliberately plotted to take Captain Robinson's life. During the delirium which preceded his last moments, Captain Robinson was haunted by the vision of the arch-brute. He imagined that Niemeyer and sentries with fixed bayonets were standing by his deathbed. Apparently Niemeyer had threatened he would avenge the death of Captain Schramm, who perished in the Zeppelin [sic] destroyed by Captain Robinson at Cuffley.

'Mrs Whipple – to whom Captain Robinson was engaged to be married – was interviewed at Stanmore on Wednesday night. She said she was sure the British public would share her fury when they knew how he had been treated. The attack of influenza, she said, was not the real cause of death. He was murdered by Niemeyer, who employed every instrument of cruelty against him. When he arrived at Stanmore ten days ago

Robinson, Sowrey and an unidentified officer aboard the Prince Henry Vauxhall at Hornchurch in late 1916. The ultimate fate of the car has not been recorded, but the late Captain R. S. Stammers believed it was auctioned off to an Essex farmer after the war. (AVM Sir Frederick Sowrey)

After the investiture of his Victoria Cross, and all the resultant press attention, Robinson found it almost impossible to lead a normal life. Despite being allowed to wear 'mufti' he was recognized wherever he went and frequently mobbed. He is seen here with Freddie Sowrey at Hornchurch. (AVM Sir Frederick Sowrey)

Visitors to Suttons Farm were frequent, and after Robinson, Sowrey and Tempest brought down three airships, the aerodrome became a virtual Mecca for scores of well-wishers, many of these being adoring young women. Robinson apparently regarded all the attention with good-humoured indifference. (AVM Sir Frederick Sowrey)

Captain R. S. Stammers, Freddie Sowrey and Robinson stroll down a lane in Hornchurch for the benefit of press photographers. The 'swagger' sticks the airmen carry were almost de rigueur for young Royal Flying Corps officers of the period and today are eagerly sought after by collectors of aeronautica. (AVM Sir Frederick Sowrey)

Robinson's sense of humour is reflected in this photograph as he breaks into a comic walk for the benefit of the cameraman; Stammers and Sowrey look on in bemusement. Though confirmation is lacking, the picture was probably taken in the grounds of Harrow Weald House, Stanmore. (MRS R. G. LIBIN)

Robinson, Sowrey and Tempest (at right) with Captain Stammers. Following Robinson's successful attack on SL11 Sowrey shot down the Zeppelin L32 over Billericay on the night of 24 September, 1916, and Tempest destroyed L31 over Potters Bar on 2 October — both airman received DSOs for their actions. (AVM SIR FREDERICK SOWREY)

'With all my heart I am thinking of you Dear Captain Robinson.' The popular Parisienne actress and singer Mademoiselle Alice Delysia won many admirers at the Moulin Rouge and the Folies Bergère. During 1916 she was appearing in a revue in the West End and became a frequent visitor to Suttons Farm. (Mrs R. G. Libin)

A familiar studio portrait of the modest 'Hero of Cuffley'. Robinson was taken off flying duties following his near-disastrous crash on the night of 16 September and, much against his wishes, his time was spent on an almost constant round of official engagements. (Mrs R. G. Libin)

The night fliers of No.
39 HDS. Standing
(left to right) are
Captain Robert
Sidney Stammers;
Second Lieutenant
Wulstan Joseph
Tempest DSO;
Lieutenants William
Leefe Robinson, VC;
Frederick Sowrey,
DSO, and Major A.
H. Morton. Seated
are Lieutenants C. C.
G. Brock, C. C.
Durston and P. R.
Mallinson. (AVM
Sir Frederick
Sowrey)

Another, somewhat less informal,
pose for the press photographers as
Robinson steps from an RFC Crossley
tender at Hornchurch. Pictures such
as these filled the popular papers for
weeks after Robinson's destruction of
SL11 and virtually his every move was
reported to an adoring public. (Mrs R.
G. Libin)

On Saturday, 14 October, 1916, presentations were made in the NZ Camp at Grey Towers, Hornchurch, to Robinson, Sowrey and Tempest for their successful attacks on SL11, L32 and L31: the airmen were each awarded a handsome silver cup. Here, Robinson and Sowrey talk to local dignatories during the event. (AVM SIR FREDERICK SOWREY)

A less well-known portrait of Robinson, possibly taken in the grounds of Harrow Weald House, near Stanmore. Restless and frustrated at the enforced inaction his popular status demanded of him, Robinson applied several times for an overseas posting and finally succeeded in February 1917. (MRS R. G. LIBIN)

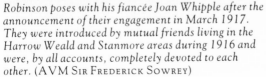

Robinson poses with his fiancée Joan Whipple after the announcement of their engagement in March 1917. They were introduced by mutual friends living in the Harrow Weald and Stanmore areas during 1916 and were, by all accounts, completely devoted to each other. (AVM SIR FREDERICK SOWREY)

Captain William Leefe Robinson, VC, stands before a new Bristol F2A Fighter, possibly at Rendcombe, Gloucestershire, in February 1917. The squadron flew out to France in March and the following month Robinson led a flight of machines for the unit's first operational sortie over the lines. (AVM SIR FREDERICK SOWREY)

Sergeant Sebastian Festner of Jagdstaffel 11 prepares for a patrol in his Albatros D.III. It was Festner who shot down Robinson and observer Lieutenant Edward Darien Warburton on 5 April, 1917, for his fourth accredited victory. Festner would bring down a further eight enemy machines before his death on 25 April, 1917. (D. WHETTON)

After capture Robinson was sent to the POW camp at Freiburg and in September 1917, together with several fellow officers, managed to escape from a window in one of the prison wings; they were later recaptured. The photograph shows the escape team and the window (marked X) from which they made their exit. (H. E. Hervey)

'Nine RFC officers who are prisoners in Germany.' The Daily Mirror *ran this photograph in their 22 August, 1917, edition which shows: (1) W. J. Hills; (2) G. C. Hicks; (3) W. L. Robinson, VC; (4) S. Roche; (5) E. J. A. Bell; (6) F. C. Craig; (7) J. S. Heagerty; (8) Arthur A. Baerlin and (9) F. E. Hills. It was Baerlin who was later court-martialled with Robinson for 'attempted bribery'. (Author's Collection)*

After four escape attempts in as many months, Robinson's reputation as a troublesome charge was growing and this, together with the fame accorded him by his destruction of SL11, often proved inconvenient to fellow escapers. As H. E. Hervey noted, 'He was considered a desperate character and guarded accordingly.' (Mrs R. G. Libin)

Robinson poses with an, as yet, unidentified officer in this official photograph taken by Oskar Brauer of Frankfurt during late 1917. Following his court martial in October, Robinson was sentenced to a month's solitary confinement in the dreaded underground fortress at Zorndorf. (Mrs R. G. Libin)

On 2 May, 1918, Robinson was transferred to Clausthal in the Harz Mountains. First impressions of the POW camp with its main building, a popular pre-war holiday resort standing on the shores of a lake, were misleading. Robinson came under the jurisdiction of Heinrich Niemeyer, who with twin brother Karl were the most notorious camp commandants in Germany. (H. E. HERVEY)

Robinson and two unidentified officers probably at Clausthal in the spring of 1918, the official photographer being Max Gunther of Coblenz. Robinson was finally transferred to Holzminden in July 1918, where the camp commandant, Karl Niemeyer, singled him out for 'ceaseless, cruel and methodical' persecution. (MRS R. DAVID)

Believed to be one of the last photographs of Captain William Leefe Robinson, VC, being taken shortly after his repatriation in December 1918. His expression reflects his poor state of health at the time and while spending Christmas with friends at Stanmore he fell victim to the worldwide influenza pandemic. (MRS R. G. LIBIN)

Robinson died at Stanmore on 31 December with his friends Noel and Nancie Clifton and Joan at the bedside. The funeral of the 'Cuffley VC' took place during the afternoon of 3 January, 1919. Here, the cortège moves slowly down Uxbridge Road preceded by the Central Band of the RAF. (C. Rust)

The procession nears All Saints Church. The Daily Sketch later reported: 'Only his relatives and a few intimate friends and chosen comrades of the air attended the hero's body to the grave. But the women and children to whom he brought a sense of safety made an informal guard of honour.' (Author's Collection)

Major Frederick Sowrey, DSO (left), and Major Noel Clifton were among the bearers who shouldered the coffin to the far corner of the small cemetery in Harrow Weald. Before the ceremony a formation of fighter aeroplanes led by Brigadier Higgins dropped a large laurel wreath from the 6th Brigade RAF. (Author's Collection)

The grave of Captain W. L. Robinson, VC, at Harrow Weald upon which flowers are regularly placed by staff of the Leefe Robinson restaurant sited on the opposite side of Uxbridge Road, which flanks the small cemetery. Every Armistice Day St Bees School sends a wreath of poppies. (Author)

At 15.30 hours on 9 June, 1921, a memorial stone to Captain W. L. Robinson, VC, was unveiled at Cuffley close to the spot where SL11 crashed to earth. The obelisk was erected following subscriptions raised by Daily Express readers, the open meadow site being presented by Mrs J. M. Kidston of nearby Nyn Park, Northaw. (Mrs R. G. Libin)

The memorial at East Ridgeway, Cuffley, photographed by the author in 1975. When first unveiled the stone carried an erroneous reference to 'L21', but due to efforts of local historian Michael Clark in the 1960s the inscription was subsequently changed to give the correct designation of SL11. (Author)

On Tuesday, 3 September, 1986, at 18.00 hours the Cuffley memorial was unveiled for the second time following a restoration organized by the Welwyn Hatfield District Council due to the original stone being vandalized. The ceremony was well attended, the unveiling being undertaken by Air Vice Marshal M. J. D. Stear, CBE, MA, RAF. (AUTHOR)

One of the most popular restaurants in the area, Berni's Leefe Robinson at Harrow Weald, Middlesex, stands at the other side of Uxbridge Road opposite the graveyard of All Saints Church, where Captain W. L. Robinson, VC, is buried. Whitbreads, the restaurant owners, ensure the grave is regularly tended. (AUTHOR)

On 14 November, 1988, during Christie's two-day exhibition of Robinson memorabilia at the Leefe Robinson restaurant, 93-year-old Squadron Leader H. E. Hervey posed for photographers at the graveside of his former POW comrade. He is seen here with Richard Bishop, associate director of Christie's Coins and Medals department. (AUTHOR)

Robinson's VC went to an anonymous English collector at Christie's on 22 November, 1988, for £99,000. Sold along with the medal were Robinson's personal papers and photographs as well as several pieces of the airship SL11. The proceeds of the sale funded 'A Medal for Life', the charitable trust which benefits children suffering from Leukaemia. (AUTHOR)

he was too broken to resist the slightest cold. As one instance of cruelty, Mrs Whipple said for six whole weeks he was placed in solitary confinement. No light, fuel or even as much as a smoke. Sentries dogged his footsteps. They jeered and scoffed at him. They outraged him in every possible fashion.

'Baroness Heyking said that when her brother returned to England he never spoke a single word of his terrible sufferings. The whole ghastly story came out in his delirium. It was solitary confinement which killed him. The guards stole his parole [sic] and cigarettes. In three months he only had two parcels. They mocked and jeered him in the most outrageous fashion and made his life a hell.'[4]

Tryggve Gran provided further confirmation of William's final sufferings:

'In his feverish hallucinations Robinson once more returned to the torments of the prison camp. "They hit me, they hit me", he cried until the very last moment of his life.'[5]

Considering how many fit young men died during the pandemic there is little reason to suppose that Robinson, once having contracted the disease, would have survived even if he had been in the rudest of health. In any event the official view went against the women's wishes and nothing was ever done about either of the Niemeyers, although there were unofficial moves to gain a measure of revenge. At least one ex-Holzminden inmate remained in Europe determined to track down 'Milwaukee Bill', but the ambitious plan came to nothing and the twins appear simply to have vanished. Some ex-POWs claimed Karl Niemeyer was shot, others that he committed suicide. The real truth may never be known.[6]

William Leefe Robinson was buried on 3 January, 1919, at 2.30 pm, his coffin being laid to rest at the farthest corner of Wealdstone Cemetery, the nearest point to where 'he had spent many happy hours'. It was a full military affair and thousands attended in scenes reminiscent of those at Cuffley three years earlier when the mood was one of elation rather than grief.

Brigadier Higgins' flypast of fighter aeroplanes opened the proceedings which were as impressive as they were moving. At the head of the cortège which proceeded from Gordon Avenue was the Band of the Central Royal Air Force followed at a respectable distance by an RAF tender towing a trailer upon which the coffin, bedecked with a huge Union Flag and masses of floral tributes had been laid. The trailer was escorted by air force officers from the stations at Northolt and Hounslow and met at the church gates by the local vicar, Reverend H. Van Cooten, and Reverend Basil Phillips, the RAF chaplain. The coffin was shouldered by six RAF officers: Major Clifton, Captains Evans, Hamming, Selwyn and Wilkens and Major Frederick Sowrey, DSO, MC, for whom it was a particularly poignant moment.

Once inside All Saints Church, the mourners shuffled into their places in the pews and the hymn books were taken up. So many of the dead airman's relatives and friends were gathered there on either side of the coffin as it rested in the aisle. Apart from the Heykings and Joan there was Aunt Constance; cousin Reginald Braham Robinson; Reverend G. R. Leefe (the Vicar of Ringmer); Reverend F. E. Sturgess (the Vicar of Yiewsley); Nancie Clifton; members of the Grinling family: Harry, Sydney and Violet;

Mrs Stapleton-Smyth; the Mayor of Harrow, Mr R. Blair, MP, and his wife and, representing Lord Weir, Colonel Steele-Ferkins.

The Reverend Phillips conducted the service, and two of Robinson's favourite hymns, 'For All The Saints' and 'Fight The Good Fight', were sung before the coffin was lifted again and followed out of the church by the congregation. Friends and relatives gathered around the graveside as the casket was lowered into position following committal prayers. The Last Post was sounded by Sergeant Major Murrell, Chief Trumpeter of the RAF, as the large crowd slowly began to disperse. *The Harrow Observer*'s reporter was particularly impressed by the many floral tributes placed around the grave:

'The wreaths were exceedingly beautiful. Just before the cortège started the flight of aeroplanes encircled Lavender Cottage and one dropped a giant wreath of laurel. It fell with remarkable precision in front of the dwelling, was picked up and placed on the coffin within. This was from the officer commanding and officers of the 6th Brigade, RAF. One tribute was a lustrous cross of orchids and violets, bearing on it a single word, "Joan"[7] – and another from Baroness Heyking, a cross of lilies, amelias and violets: "To the sacred memory of my gallant brother, in ever-living love and devotion – Kitty."'[8]

The number of wreaths around the graveside was indeed breathtaking, not only from the family but from friends like the Cliftons, the Grinlings and from St Bees, Robinson's old school, who, over 70 years later, still send flowers to the grave every Armistice Day.

In his will William Leefe Robinson left £2346 and nine shillings, which was distributed between his father and Kitty. Horace and 'Bessie' Robinson left Pollibetta after 'The Great War' and made their last home at No. 83 Woodcote Road (Dalnabreck), a large and imposing house in Wallington formerly occupied by Kitty and her husband Baron Heyking. There on 23 February, 1929, at the age of 77, Elizabeth Robinson died and her beloved Horace followed her in death just eight weeks later.[9] They are buried in one grave at Bandon Hill Cemetery, Beddington, in Surrey.

EPILOGUE

November 11, Armistice Day. It is a cold, crisp morning and the sky is a clear cobalt. The visitor crosses Uxbridge Road, which is strangely quiet on this special Sunday morning. The old wooden cemetery gates have long since disappeared, and wandering down the leaf-strewn path, bordered by rampant weeds and unchecked brambles that snag every step, the whole scene is one of decay. The keen wind whistles eerily through the branches of gaunt trees that stand like emaciated sentinels over the tumbled, vandalized gravestones which lie forlorn in seemingly meaningless array. Entire families are buried here; old soldiers and one-time local notaries, now just so many forgotten names etched on crumbling granite.

As rustling leaves play around the visitor's feet, a splash of unexpected colour suddenly arrests his attention. Set in the far corner of the graveyard, over to the right, is an impressive stone cross, beneath it an inscribed border. The grave is singularly free of neglect. There's a spray of fresh flowers in a metal urn; beyond, a large wreath of poppies is propped against the headstone and weeds are conspicuous by their absence. On the wreath is attached a small white card: 'In grateful memory from St Bees School, Cumbria.' The 'Old St Beghians' do this every year and have done so since the early 1920s; the school does not forget its 'old boy' heroes. On Saturday, 18 June, 1932, a special tablet was unveiled in St Bees' chapel to commemorate the school's three 'Great War' VC recipients: William Leefe Robinson, John Fox Russell and Richard Leslie Wain. Several momentoes of Robinson are still cherished by St Bees, including his rugger cap and the imposing silver cup awarded him by the residents of Hornchurch over seven decades ago.

Visitors to Cuffley may seek out the recently-restored *Daily Express* memorial which stands on East Ridgeway not far from the Plough public house. The site for the large monument was donated by Mrs J. M. B. Kidston of Nyn Park, Northaw, and the unveiling took place on Thursday, 9 June, 1921, by the Right Honourable F. E. Guest, CBE, DSO, MP, the then Secretary for Air, to large crowds.

Perhaps the most well-known 'memorial' to Robinson is the restaurant at Brockhurst Corner that lies opposite the little graveyard at Harrow Weald and bears the famous name over its broad entrance. Originally it was 'The Leefe Robinson Restaurant', whose proprietor, Mr Ted Hulks, opened his doors for business on 21 June, 1954. The establishment quickly acquired an enviable reputation, boasting an exceptionally fine menu and an impressive wine cellar. Many relics relating to Robinson were displayed, including a BE2c airscrew, but this and many other historical items were lost following a disastrous fire in the 1960s. Rebuilt as a Berni Inn, 'The Leefe Robinson' is today one of the most popular restaurants in the area and heavily patronized. Some of the items displayed on the saloon bar walls include Robinson's autograph, scraps of airship metal, and a selection of photographs – some relevant, others like a picture of *R100* and the wrecked Zeppelin *L48* at Theberton, somewhat less so. A long-standing stipulation in the lease from Whitbreads ensures that Robinson's grave is regularly maintained and that fresh flowers are placed there, this gesture for many years being undertaken by Jack Roseigh, the restaurant's resident gardener.

Almost 70 years after his tragic and untimely death, William Leefe Robinson made newspaper headlines once more when, in September 1988, Mrs Regina Libin decided to auction her uncle's historic Victoria Cross and related memorabilia which her family had treasured for so many years. The mass of material included a great deal of personal correspondence as well as a large number of rare photographs, all of which have played an important part in research for this book. Following heavy media coverage generated by London auctioneers Christie's, which included several well-attended exhibitions at key venues around the country, Robinson's VC went under the gavel on 22 November, 1988, and realized £99,000. The new owner was a 'private English collector' whose identity is unlikely to be revealed.

The entire proceeds of the sale were used to fund 'A Medal for Life', the charitable trust set up by Gia Libin to aid children suffering from Leukaemia, providing them with holidays and financing new research to help combat the deadly disease. The charity represents a fitting and lasting memorial to one of 'The Great War's' most celebrated air heroes, whose life story can now be concluded on a positive note in the knowledge that his award-winning achievement of many decades ago will now benefit the living in many more decades to come . . .

Mors Janua Vitae

APPENDIX I

Air Raid Statistics, 3 September, 1916

876001/1412

SUMMARY of particulars of the hostile Air Raid over Metropolitan Police District on 3rd September, 1916.

The airship was first seen at 1.20 am 3rd. when a Zeppelin passed over Enfield, travelling NW. The engines were clearly heard.

At 1.48 am, aircraft machinery was heard by Police at Walthamstow still travelling NW. At 2.05 am the airship was *seen* from Stoke Newington lit up by searchlights and it passed N. At 2.09 am the airship was seen from Leman Street Police Station travelling S at a great height and appeared to be slightly N of High St. Shoreditch. It was immediately picked up by searchlights and heavily bombarded when it turned E then NE. At 2.10 the airship passed over Hackney, the noise of the engines being distinctly heard, and turned N after being heavily bombarded. All Divisions concerned report that the airship burst into flames at 2.20 am. Supt. Y recording the incident as follows:

'At 2.20 am a Zepp. was seen at Northaw, Potters Bar, travelling in a north-east direction followed by an aeroplane, carrying a light underneath. The aeroplane fired at the Zepp. and immediately the airship caught fire at a height of about 3000 feet and fell to the earth a mass of flames in a field at Castle Farm, Cuffley.' 15 bodies [*sic*] of the crew burnt beyond recognition were recovered from the debris. A military guard of Royal Horse Guards attended from Albany St. Barracks.

The atmosphere is given as
(H) clear; no wind perceptible.
(Y) misty, with heavy ground fog.[1]

101

SUMMARY OF CASUALTIES AND DAMAGE

Divisions concerned	Districts affected	Bombs Dropped		Casualties		Total	Damage
		Ex.	Inc.	Killed M.W.C.	Injured M.W.C.		
H.	Leman St. and Shoreditch	–	–	– – –	– – –		Nil
J.	Hackney.	–	–	– – –	– – –		Slight damage to roofs of 2 houses by fragments of AA shells.
N.	Edmonton. Tottenham. Ponders End. Enfield Highway. Walthamstow. Goffs Oak.	24	3	– – –	– 1 –	1	Roadway and water main badly damaged at High St. Ponders End; tram and telephone wires broken and 63 houses damaged. Greenhouses and 14 houses damaged at Enfield Highway, 3 houses damaged in Turkey St. Damage elsewhere on N nil.
S.	Shenley. London Colney. South Mimms. Regents Park.	5	5	– – –	– – –		Nil.
Y.	Southgate. Northaw. Clayhill. East Barnet. Bulls Cross. Enfield. Potters Bar.	11	16	– – –	– – –		Stable and outbuildings burnt out at Clayhill. 3 valuable horses killed. Bombs fell in fields at Bulls Cross and elsewhere; no damage.
		40	24	– – –	– 1 –	– 1	

APPENDIX II

Home Defence Summary, 5 September, 1916

SECRET

HEADQUARTERS.
Home Defence Wing,
Royal Flying Corps.

General Headquarters.

HOME DEFENCE WING
ROYAL FLYING CORPS
No. HD/58a
Date 5.9.16

Home Forces.

....

Report of action taken – Hostile Air Raid
September 2nd – 3rd 1916

....

I attach herewith summary of action taken by Squadrons during raid by Hostile Aircraft on the night of 2nd – 3rd September:

No. 33 HD Squadron.
Acting on information received one machine left the ground from Beverley.
Captain R. C. L. Holme on BE2c 2661 started at 12.55, but crashed getting off. The pilot was unhurt.
No other action was taken by this Squadron.

No. 36 HD Squadron
No action taken.

No. 38 HD Squadron
No action taken.

No. 39 HD Squadron
Acting on information received six machines left the ground. Lieut. W. L. Robinson on a BE2c left the ground at Suttons Farm 11.10 pm to patrol between Suttons Farm and Joyce Green. At about 1.10 am when at a height of 12,900 feet he saw a Zeppelin in the searchlight SE of Woolwich. He at once gave chase and judging it to be only 800 feet below him, he sacrificed speed in order to keep his height.

After about ten minutes he lost sight of the Zeppelin, which had evaded the searchlight by entering clouds, and returned to his patrol.

At 2.5 am he sighted a Zeppelin over NNE London in the searchlight and saw shells bursting, also night tracer shells, and made with all speed in this direction. When he got closer he noticed the AA gun fire was either too high or too low, a number of shells were bursting 800 feet behind the Zeppelin also. When about 800 feet below the Zeppelin he flew along its length from bow to stern firing one drum, this appeared to have no effect, and then he distributed another drum along its side, again with no apparent effect. His height was now 11,500 feet and he judged the Zeppelin to be about 500 feet above him.

He next concentrated the fire of a whole drum on one place in the rear of the Zeppelin and underneath, and had hardly finished firing before the part fired at commenced to glow, and in a few seconds the whole of the rear part of the Zeppelin was ablaze. When firing the last drum there were no AA guns firing and the Zeppelin was not in the searchlight.

He landed at Suttons Farm at 2.45 am.

Lieut. *Ross* on BE12 6484 left North Weald Bassett at 11.11 pm to patrol North Weald Bassett to Hainault Farm. He patrolled till 1 am seeing no hostile aircraft, he then had a forced landing on his own aerodrome crashing the machine. The pilot was unhurt.

Lieut. *Brandon* on BE2c 2090 left the ground 11.12 pm from Hainault Farm to patrol Hainault Farm to Suttons Farm. The pilot reached a height of 9900 feet but saw no hostile aircraft, and landed at 1.38 am at Hainault Farm.

Lieut. *Sowrey* left the ground from Suttons Farm at 1.7 am to patrol Joyce Green to Farningham. At a height of 2500 feet he had engine failure and landed at Suttons Farm at 1.20 am.

Lieut. *MacKay* on BE2c 2574 left the ground from North Weald Bassett at 1.8 am to patrol, to the river at Joyce Green. When at a height of 8000 feet he observed AA fire and proceeded in the direction of it, he saw no hostile aircraft. He then returned in the direction of Joyce Green, climbing to 10,000 feet. When about Joyce Green he observed a Zeppelin in the searchlight North of London, and gave chase. He held it in view for about 25 minutes and by this time had approached within a mile of it, when it fell in flames.

He then returned towards Joyce Green and saw another Zeppelin NE of Hainault Farm, after a fifteen minutes chase he lost sight of it and resumed his patrol.

He landed at North Weald Bassett at 4.10 am.

Lieut. *Hunt* on BE2c 2727 from Hainault Farm left the ground at 1.22 am to patrol Joyce Green to Farningham. When at a height of 10,000 feet about 2.10 am he saw a Zeppelin in the searchlight, which he judged to be about 800 feet above him. He at once gave chase, climbing his machine. When approaching to attack, the Zeppelin suddenly burst into flames, and passed in this condition within 200 yards of his machine. In the blaze of light he saw another Zeppelin about ¼ of a mile away and 1000 feet lower, which he at once pursued but lost sight of almost immediately as the Zeppelin left the lighted area, and he was dazzled by the glare.

The pilot had now lost his bearings but continued patrolling and half an hour later saw another Zeppelin this time about 2000 feet above him. It disappeared in a westerly direction and he followed but lost sight of it. He landed at Hainault Farm at 3.44 am.

No. 50 HD Squadron

Acting on information received 3 machines left the ground about 11.30 pm.

Captain Woodhouse on BE2c 4588 left the ground 11.30 pm and patrolled for two hours between Dover and North Foreland reaching a height of 9000 feet. He saw nothing and landed at Marston.

Captain Sowrey on BE2c 2711 was compelled to return almost immediately with engine trouble.

2/Lieut. Fraser patrolled in the vicinity of Dover at 6000 feet but seeing nothing landed at Dover after 1 hour 55 minutes.

(Signed) F. R. Hedges,
Captain.
for Lieut. Colonel.
Commanding, Home Defence Wing,
Royal Flying Corps.

Adastral House,
Victoria Embankment, E.C.
5th September 1916 [2]

APPENDIX III

Report on Night Patrol, 2/3 September, 1916

Confidential

From: Lieut. Robinson,
Suttons Farm.

To: The Officer Commanding,
39 HD Squadron.

Sir,

I have the honour to make the following report on Night Patrol made by me on the night of the 2nd-3rd instant. I went up at about 11.8 pm on the night of the 2nd with instructions to patrol between Suttons Farm and Joyce Green.

I climbed to 10,000 feet in 53 minutes, I counted what I thought were ten sets of flares — there were a few clouds below me but on the whole it was a beautifully clear night.

I saw nothing till 1.10 am when two searchlights picked up a Zeppelin about SE of Woolwich. The clouds had collected in this quarter, and the searchlights had some difficulty in keeping on the aircraft.

By this time I had managed to climb to 12,900 feet, and I made in the direction of the Zeppelin, which was being fired on by a few anti-aircraft guns — hoping to cut it off on its way eastward. I very slowly gained on it for about ten minutes — I judged it to be about 800 feet below me, and I sacrificed my speed in order to keep the height. It went behind some clouds avoided the searchlights and I lost sight of it. After 15 minutes' fruitless search I returned to my patrol.

I managed to pick up and distinguish my flares again.

At about 1.50 am I noticed a red glow in NE London. Taking it to be an outbreak of fire I went in that direction.

At 2.5 am a Zeppelin was picked up by the searchlights over NNE London (as far as I could judge).

Remembering my last failure I sacrificed height (I was still 12,900 feet) for speed and made nose down in the direction of the Zeppelin. I saw shells bursting and night tracer shells flying around it. When I drew closer I noticed that the anti-aircraft aim was too high or too low; also a good many some 800 feet behind — a few tracers went right over. I could hear the bursts when about 3000 feet from the Zeppelin.

I flew about 800 feet below it from bow to stern and distributed one drum along it (alternate New Brock and Pomeroy). It seemed to have no effect; I therefore moved to one side and gave it another drum distributed along its side — without apparent effect. I then got behind it (by this time I was very close – 500 feet or less below) and concentrated one drum on one part (underneath rear). I was then at a height of 11,500 feet when attacking Zeppelin.

I hardly finished the drum before I saw the part fired at glow. In a few seconds the whole rear part was blazing.

When the third drum was fired there were no searchlights on the Zeppelin and no anti-aircraft was firing.

I quickly got out of the way of the falling, blazing Zeppelin and being very excited fired off a few red Very's lights and dropped a parachute flare.

Having very little oil and petrol left I returned to Suttons Farm, landing at 2.45 am.

On landing I found I had shot away the machine gun wire guard, the rear part of the centre section, and had pierced the rear main spar several times.

> I have the honour to be, Sir,
> Your obedient Servant,
> > (Sgd) W. L. Robinson, Lieut.
> > No. 39 Squadron, RFC[3]

APPENDIX IV

Notes on Documents and Relics Recovered from SL11

1. *Urlaubskarte. Gefreiter* Jeziorski.v. *Komdo. SL11.*
   (leave for Siegburg, Spich sheds, August. Signed Schramm.)
2. *Urlaubskarte. Gefreiter* Jeziorski, leave Hannover. Signed Schramm.
3-7. Four receipts for telegraphic money payments: two issued at Lipine (Poland) for Jeziorski, *and* two at Niedergoersdorf (Jüterbog) for *Gefreiter* Koopman, *Schulkomo*, Niedergoersdorf. One of the latter has the stamp of the *Luftschiff Kommando.*
8. Receipt to Jeziorski for supplementary bread-money (*Britgeldzuschuss*) for leave period 21-26 April signed *Feldwebel.*
9. Doctor's prescription (Liegnitz.)
10. Bookseller's receipt for 1*m*.80 *pf*, Stuttgart.
11. Three Cologne tram tickets.
12. Telegraphic money receipt issued at Bad Kosen.
13. *Urlaubskarte* for *Obersteuermann* Sendzick issued in Siegburg, 1 September and signed Seitz, *Lnt.*
14. Ditto for same man to Alberstadt and Köln and Ober-Roplingen a/see. Spich, 17 August. Signed Schramm. (*Luftschiffertruppe* 19 in Spich).
15. 50 *Mark* note from purse of *Obermaschinist* Porath.
16. 5 *Mark* note, *Darlehenskassenschein* (from purse of Sendzick).
17. 2 *Mark* note, *Darlehenskassenschein* (from purse of Sendzick).
18. 2 *Mark* note, *Darlehenskassenschein* (from purse of Sendzick).
19. *Urlaubskarte* for *Obermaschinist* Porath from Hannover 6 June. Signed Schramm.
20. *Urlaubskarte* for *Obermaschinist* Porath from Spich 28 August.
21. *Urlaubskarte* for *Obermaschinist* Porath from Hannover.
22. *Urlaubskarte* for *Obermaschinist* Porath from Hannover signed Lempertz, *Oberleutnant.*
23. *Urlaubskarte* for *Obermaschinist* Porath from Hannover (stamped *LZ93*).
24. Doctor's prescription for *Herr* Lorenz, 10.7.16.
25. Receipt Berlin, 10.7.16.
26. Fragment of a postal order issued to *Frau* ... wede ..., 1 Strasse (?) Warnemunde.
27. Address of Thirza Jaeschke and Elsa Scharff.

28. Address of Harry Stringer (?) Berlin.
29. Address of Helen Stremm, Berlin Mullerstrasse.
30. Piece of tissue paper with fragment of shrapnel bullet.
31. Picture postcard stuck to cover of a notebook from Wolsdorf, Papageistrasse, Tilde Schup – addressed to *Obermaschinist* Baumann.
32. Letter to Baumann at Spich, 31 August, 1916 (inc. envelope).
33. Letter to Baumann stating that the writer's family is short of milk and fat and she thanks him for sending bread-ticket.
34. Four 20 *Mark* notes ⎤
    Three 5 *Mark* notes ⎟
    Two 2 *Mark* notes ⎬ in a purse.
    One 1 *Mark* note ⎦
35. Two newspaper fragments.
36. Purse with a monogram *L1* and a miniature Iron Cross (lost).
37. Fragment of a map of Central Europe.
38. Identification disc without number.
39. A weather report transmitted (?W/T) from Hannover.
40. Pass issued to Porath signed by Lempertz and Schramm dated July 1916 Nr. 7.
41. An IOU (?) for 1.50 *pf* dated August 8 (name on it, Boysen).
42. Slip of paper with writing ? an address ? of Hoffmann (Meyer).
43. 2 coins (5 *pf*) and a key.
45. Four-page letter on black edge notepaper seems to be written in a melancholy strain and to deal with family matters.
46. Meat tickets.
47. Slip of paper apparently with name and address (not decipherable) in indelible pencil.
48. Notebook, blank except for front page, which has certain airship calculations.
49. Fragments of a linen-backed map or chart on squared paper.
50. Fur-lined leather aviator's helmet; name inside, Hassenmüller.
51. Cap, field grey, with black velvet band, red piping and peak as worn by Pioneers.
52. Silver Hunter (stopped at 3.27-glass and dial broken, face bent by concussion) piece of vest adhering to it. (Claimed by Lnt. Robinson). Reported to belong to an officer.
53. Rosary (black beads) with brass crucifix.
54. Small brass crucifix (? Rosary cross).
55. Iron Cross unsoldered in three pieces badly bent (? by concussion) reported to belong to an officer.
56. Swiss watch (nickel and brass-embossed back with 16″ long brass chain). Stopped at 3.15. Glass broken, dial cracked . . . otherwise in good condition.
57. Nickel Silver watch (by Reinecke of Prenzlau) luminous dial stopped at 3.34.
58. Gun metal watch with swivel and a few links of chain, showing effects of fire. Stopped at half past three?
59. Watch (Silver?) with second hand stopped at 3.20 – badly charred.

60. Watch (Silver?) in porcelain face and glass in a semi-molten state.
61. Watch (Silver?) in gunmetal protective case. Stopped at 12.28.
62. Bible 8vo published in Zurich 1808. Velvet binding, brass mounts and clasps.
63. Linen label, cut out from lining of a tunic, typewritten inside is *Maschinist* Baerenlaut *LZ77*.
64. Plain gold ring reported to belong to commander of *SL11*, engraved inside is *A.O. Pfingster 1913* = (Whitsuntide).
65. Large watch (two and a half inches diameter) from the front gondola of *SL11*. Stopped at 3.23. Glass broken – maker Ludwig Lerbach, Munchen.

Note: Certain documents not set forth above were handed to the DID. These included a log-book, and list of wireless messages received on board. A copy (?) by a German, of an article in French dealing with conditions at Salonika.[4]

APPENDIX V

The Roll of Honour, SL11, 3 September, 1916

Rank	Name	Date of Birth	Birthplace
Obermaschinist	Jakob Baumann	3.7.1887	Nordach
Leutnant	Hans Geitel	6.6.1892	Berlin
Vizefeldwebel	Rudolf Goltz	24.7.1881	Koschmin
Feldwebel Leutnant	Paul Hassenmüller	5.7.1887	St Johann
Gefreiter	Bernard Jeziorski	3.5.1892	Schlesien
Untermaschinist	Fritz Jourdan	9.5.1892	Pforzheim
Untermaschinist	Karl Kächele	24.2.1894	Blaubeuren
Obersteuermann	Fritz Kopischke	2.7.1891	Prenzlau
Obermaschinist	Friedrich Mödinger	24.7.1886	Strümpfelbach
Obermaschinist	Reinhold Porath	5.9.1892	Randow
Unteroffizier	Heinrich Schlichting	26.5.1891	Bielefeld
Hauptmann	Wilhelm Schramm	11.12.1885	London
Obersteuermann	Rudolf Sendzick	8.3.1891	Berlin
Unteroffizier	Anton Tristam	28.1.1889	Witzenhausen
Oberleutnant der Reserve	Wilhelm Vohdin	8.7.1882	Widdern
Untermaschinist	Hans Winkler	28.5.1892	Calau[5]

Appendix VI

Letter from William Leefe Robinson to his parents
describing the events of 2/3 September, 1916

22 October, 1916

My darling Mother and Father,

I do really feel ashamed for not writing to you darling old people before, but still, there it is – you know what I am.

Busy!! Heavens, for the last 7 weeks I have done enough to last anyone a lifetime. It has been a wonderful time for me!

I won't say much about 'strafing' the Zepp L21 for two reasons; to begin with most of it is strictly secret and secondly I'm really so tired of the subject and telling people about it, that I feel as if I never want to mention it again – so I will only say a very few words about it.

When the colossal thing actually burst into flames of course it was a *glorious* sight – wonderful! It literally lit up all the sky around and me as well of course. I saw my machine as in the firelight and sat still half dazed staring at the wonderful sight before me, not realizing to the least degree the wonderful thing that had happened!

My feelings? *Can* I describe my feelings? I hardly know how I felt as I watched the huge mass gradually turn on end and – as it seemd to me – slowly sink, one glowing blazing mass. I gradually realized what I had done and grew wild with excitement. When I had cooled down a bit, I did what I don't think many people would think I would do, and that was thanked God with all my heart. You darling old mother and father, I'm not what is popularly known as a religious person, but on occasions such as that one must realize a little how one does trust in providence. I felt an overpowering feeling of thankfulness, so it was strange that I should pause and think for a moment after the first 'blast' of excitement as it were, was over and thank from the bottom of my heart, that supreme power that rules and guides our destinies?

When I reached the ground once more, I was greeted with, 'was it you Robin', etc. etc. 'Yes, I've Strafed the beggar this time', I said, whereupon the whole flight set up a yell and carried me out of my machine to the office – cheering like mad.

Talking of cheering, they say it was wonderful to hear all London cheering – people who have heard thousands of huge crowds cheering before say they have heard nothing like it. When Sowrey and Tempest brought down their Zepps I had an opportunity of hearing something like it, although they say it wasn't as grand as mine, which could be heard twenty and even thirty miles outside London.

It swelled and sank, first one quarter of London, then *millions* of throats giving vent to thousands of feelings.

I would give anything for you dear people to have heard it. A moment before dead silence (for the guns had ceased to fire at it) then this outburst. The relief, the thanks, the gratitude of millions of people. All the sirens, hooters and whistles of steam engines, boats on the river, and munition and other works all joined in and literally filled the air – and the cause of it all – little me sitting in my little aeroplane above 13,000 feet of darkness!!

– it's wonderful – !

And to think that I should be chosen to be the recipient of the thanks of all England! (For that's what it amounts to.)

Dear old G who will be with you when you receive this will tell you something of the letters and telegrams I have received. The day after I was awarded the VC I received 37 telegrams, which includes one from my colonel and one from General Henderson, who is of course, the boss of the whole RFC.

I have had tons of interviews too, amongst which are those I have had with – The Grand Duke Michle (???!) of Russia, Lord Curzon, General Sir David Henderson and heaps of others. When I went to Windsor to get the VC, the King was awfully nice, asked me all about you dear people and Grandfather etc., and showed me some awfully interesting photographs taken from the air over the German lines.

G will tell you all about the 4 days leave I had at Southbourne with her. Oh, I could go on telling you what I have done and go on writing for a month of Sundays but I must cut things short. I have of course had hundreds of invitations most of which I have had to refuse owing to duty.

I went up to Newcastle for a day and was entertained by the Lord Mayor who gave a dinner in my honour, when I was presented with a cheque for £2000 by Col. Cowen of Newcastle. They wanted to make the whole thing a grand public function but HQ wouldn't let them, for which I was very thankful.

I've had endless other small presents – some of the nicest are paintings of the burning Zepp. By-the-by about 5 artists have offered to paint my portrait for the RA.

As I daresay you have seen in the papers – babies, flowers and hats have been named after me also poems and prose have been dedicated to me – oh, it's too much!

I am recognized wherever I go about Town now, whether in uniform or mufti – The city police salute me – The waiters, Hall porters and pages of Hotels and Restaurants bow and scrape – visitors turn round and stare – oh, it's *too* thick!

But the most glorious thing is that Sowrey, dear old boy, and Tempest, sweet soul, the other two Zepp Strafers who have been awarded the DSOs are *both* in my flight!! *Some* flight – five officers, of which there are *two* DSOs and a VC and *three* Zepps to our credit – *some* record!!!

Well you darlings I'll cease now or else I'll go babbling on all night and I'm really tired.

I'll just tell you I'm not at present in Hornchurch, I'm somewhere in England on a secret mission but I'm going back to dear old Suttons Farm again.

Well *do* forgive me for not writing before.

    Ever your loving son

    Billy

I'm awfully sick about dear old Ernest − I *do* hope he's alright, the worst of it I can't find out anything where I am at present.

By-the-by mother dear, I *wish* you'd fix up about me putting some money into Jack's Estates − you wrote about it last mail − I've got £3000 to invest, and its just lying idle at present.[6]

APPENDIX VII

Proceedings from the trial of Captain Robinson and Lieutenant Baerlin,
Berlin, 16 October, 1917

I visited Freiburg on 5 October, 1917, in order to be present at a trial of two British officers who were accused of having attempted to bribe one of the German *Unteroffiziere* at the *Offiziergefangenenlager* at Freiburg. The court consisted of *Oberst Leutnant* Rummel, *Kriegsgerichtsrat Dr.* Walter, *Dr.* Simons, v. Bothmer and *Hauptmann* Luppe. The accused were Captain Robinson of the RFC and Lieutenant Baerlin. The witnesses were *Unteroffiziere* Hackenjors, Kuntze, Hagen and Finter, and two British orderlies, Coulter and MacGregor. The defence was conducted by *Rechtsanwalt Dr.* Metzger of Freiburg. A German soldier acted as interpreter.

Hackenjors, the *unteroffizier* in question, was the chief witness, and after having taken the oath, made the following statement:

He was on duty at the *Offiziergefangenenlager* at Freiburg, and had in his possession the keys of several doors, including that of the main door. One morning at the beginning of August, Lieutenant Baerlin said to him with a smile: 'For £200 you will give me the key' and Captain Robinson said in the same manner: 'I will give you *Mk.* 6000. – ' Hackenjors took this for a joke, but on 12 August he discovered a hole in the wall between the room in which all kinds of sports material was stored, and the sacristy of the church. As Hackenjors was of the opinion that Baerlin had the key of this room, as he had once given him this key, he came to the conclusion that it was no longer a joke, but that Baerlin really did mean to attempt to escape. He therefore reported the matter immediately to the commandant, informing him at the same time of Captain Robinson's remark. On 22 September, these two officers with four others made an attempt to escape, and succeeded in reaching the Swiss frontier where they were captured.

The other witnesses merely had minor details to relate. The two officers pleaded not guilty and denied having made the alleged offer and in support of their contention stated that it would have been a ridiculous offer to make as the key of the door in question was of no use to them because in making use of this exit they would have to pass the main guard, and that therefore there could be no possible chance of escape this way.

The Prosecutor said that this was not merely an attempt at bribery, as stated in the accusation, but that, in accordance with paragraph 333 *Reichsstrafgesetzbuch*, it was an absolute case of bribery for which no mitigated circumstances could be pleaded.

He therefore demanded that both the officers be sentenced to three months' imprisonment.

Rechtsanwalt Dr. Metzger, who took the greatest interest in the case, very cleverly defended the accused. Firstly, he submitted that there was no absolute proof of their having attempted to bribe the *unteroffizier* in question, as the latter could only support the accusation by his own word, and both the accused had denied the charge; he suggested that it would possibly have been better for them had they admitted attempting to play a mild joke on the *unteroffizier*, in which case they would probably not have been charged, as the commandant would also have treated the whole affair as a joke. He further insinuated that Hackenjors might have misunderstood what was said to him. Secondly, he pointed out that if the accused seriously contemplated bribery, they would have done this in a much cleverer manner, especially taking into consideration the fact that Baerlin is an advocate by profession. Thirdly, he argued that the accused would not have been satisfied with just one attempt to bribe the *unteroffizier* but would have made other attempts, but as they had not done so, he could scarcely believe that they had ever made the offer with which they were charged. Fourthly, he contended that the key would not have been of any use to them, as they could not in an attempt to escape leave the building by the main door because this led them direct into the arms of the main guard. In conclusion he respectfully begged to disagree with the statement that there were no mitigating circumstances which be taken into consideration, inasmuch as he could well understand British officers in prison in Germany making an attempt to regain their freedom.

The court adjourned for a while to deliberate, during which time I had permission and took the opportunity of talking with the two officers, who seemed in very good spirits.

The court on resuming its functions sentenced Lieutenant Baerlin to three months' and Captain Robinson to one month's imprisonment.

(Signed) G. Hockstra.[7]

APPENDIX VIII

Awards Gazetted
to Captain William Leefe Robinson

Victoria Cross
Gazetted 5 September, 1916

His Majesty the King has been graciously pleased to award the Victoria Cross to the undermentioned officer:

Lieut. William Leefe Robinson

Worc. Regt. and RFC,

for most conspicuous bravery. He attacked an enemy airship under circumstances of great difficulty and danger, and sent it crashing to the ground as a flaming wreck.

He had been in the air for more than two hours, and had previously attacked another airship during his flight.

Mentioned in Despatches
25 January, 1917. (Home Service.)
16 December, 1919, 'For gallant and distinguished services'.

APPENDIX X

Aeroplanes flown by Captain William Leefe Robinson
Technical Data

Type	Engine	Span	Length	Height	Speed	Individual Machines Flown by Robinson
AVRO 504	80 hp Gnome 7-cylinder rotary	36'0"	29'5"	10'5"	Around 95 mph at ground level	763, 768, 759, 794,(504D)
BRISTOL F2A	190 hp Rolls-Royce Mk 1 (Falcon 1) 12-cylinder in line	39'3"	25'9"	9'4"	110 mph at ground level	A3337
CAUDRON G.3	80 hp Gnome 7-cylinder rotary	43'11"	21'0"	8'6"	69 mph at ground level	5254
MARTINSYDE S1	80 hp Gnome 7-cylinder rotary	27'8"	21'0"	Not known	87 mph at ground level	717, 2448, 4240, 4252, 4238, 5447, 5448
MAURICE FARMAN MF7	70 hp Renault 8-cylinder in line	51'0"	37'9"	11'0"	56 mph at ground level	2993
RAF BE2b	90 hp RAF 1a 8-cylinder in line	38'7½"	29'6½"	11'1½"	70 mph at ground level	746, 2175
RAF BE2c	90 hp RAF 1a 8-cylinder in line	37'0"	27'3"	11'1½"	Not known	2092, 2107, 2189, 2693, 4110, 4717, 5385, 5386
RAF BE2e	90 hp RAF 1a 8-cylinder in line	40'9"	27'3"	12'0"	105 mph at ground level	Unconfirmed
RAF BE8	80 hp Gnome 7-cylinder rotary	39'6"	27'3"	Not known	70 mph at ground level	423, 632, 663, 693, 727
RAF BE8a	80 hp Gnome 7-cylinder rotary	37'8½"	27'3"	10'3½"	70 mph at ground level	2139

NOTES AND SOURCES

Chapter One

1. Ernest was educated at Dover College and the RMC, Sandhurst, before being commissioned into the 1st Lincolnshire Regiment, Bangalore on 19 January, 1902. The following year he entered the Indian Army and with the 75th Carnatic Infantry served in Aden, Ceylon, Mauritius and various parts of India, until 1930 when he retired from the service. After some farming in New Zealand, Major Robinson returned to England and was appointed curator of the RASC Museum at Aldershot until the late 1950s. Living at The Sands near Farnham, Surrey, Ernest died in 1963 at the age of 80.
2. Letter: Mrs D. Barclay to author, 12 August, 1978.
3. Letter: Harold Leefe Robinson to Irene Leefe Robinson, 12 July, 1908.
4. Letter: William Leefe Robinson to his mother, undated.
5. Letter: W. L. R. to his father, 18 January, 1912.
6. Letter: W. L. R. to his mother, September 1912.
7. Letter: W. L. R. to his father, September 1912.
8. Letter: H. L. R. to I. L. R., 25 September, 1912.
9. Letter: H. L. R. to I. L. R., 24 November, 1912.
10. Letter: W. L. R. to his father, 10 January, 1913.
11. Letter: W. L. R. to his mother, 23 January, 1913.

Chapter Two

1. Letter: C. S. Cay to author, 13 May, 1976.
2. Letter: C. S. Cay to author, 24 June, 1976.
3. *Ibid.*
4. John Irwin was often referred to as Jack in family correspondence.
5. Latin for 'as it should be'.
6. Letter: W. L. R. to his mother, 3 March, 1915.
7. Letter: W. L. R. to his mother, 15 March, 1915.

Chapter Three

1. From squadron records in Public Records Office file PRO Air 1, 748/204/3/47.
2. Letter: W. L. R. to his mother, 19 April, 1915.

3. This 'lucky halfpenny' was included in the sale of Robinson's VC and other related memorabilia at Christie's on 22 November, 1988.

4. Letter: W. L. R. to his mother, 14 May, 1915.

5. Letter: H. L. R. to I. L. R., 18 September, 1915.

6. Letter: W. L. R. to his mother, 11 November, 1915.

7. The young Robinson did indeed bear a close resemblance to the famous pre-war pilot Gustav Hamel and the similarity was frequently commented on. Hamel was drowned on 23 May, 1914, when his Morane Saulnier monoplane crashed into the English Channel while *en route* from Hardelot, France, to Hendon.

8. Robinson's logbook, currently held by the Royal Air Force Museum, confirms this trip with some additional details. Robinson records that the aeroplane was BE2c 2107; he left Castle Bromwich at 11.30 hours; the passenger was a Lieutenant Payne and the curtailed flight took 70 minutes. In the remarks column, Robinson wrote, 'Landed owing to bad weather at Port Meadow. Stayed night at Mitre Hotel.'

9. Robinson's logbook reveals that the engine malfunction was due to a broken 'throttle spindle' – the airmen left Oxford at 11.00 hours. On 10 December Robinson appended a tally of his flying hours: 'Total time in air up to date, 64 hrs 46 m; (total time in air) since ticket, 61 hrs 22 m.'

10. Letter: W. L. R. to his mother, 10 December, 1915.

11. Letter: W. L. R. to his mother, 1 January, 1916.

12. The following three lines of this letter were vigorously filled in with black ink, possibly William had given full vent to his feelings but had second thoughts later.

13. 16 January according to Robinson's logbook.

14. Probably one of the early Armstrong Whitworth FK3s fitted with the 120 hp Beardmore engine.

15. The airship raid of 31 January/1 February, 1916. See Rimell, R. L.: *Zeppelin!*, pp. 45-47.

16. Letter: W. L. R. to his mother, 6 February, 1916.

Chapter Four

1. Jones, H. A.: *The War in the Air*, Vol III, p. 69.

2. *Ibid.*

3. *Ibid,* p. 70.

4. Robinson D. H.: *The Zeppelin in Combat*, p. 56.

5. Pankhurst, S.: 'I Was in London's First Air Raid', *I Was There*, December 1938, p. 466.

6. See Rimell, R. L.: *Zeppelin!*, pp. 43-44.

7. Anti-Aircraft Summary. PRO Air 1, 2293/230/1.

8. Rimell, *op. cit.* pp. 12-17.

9. Rimell, *op. cit.* pp. 62-74.

Chapter Five

1. An original ex-home defence RAF BE2c (2699) is currently on display at the Imperial War Museum in Lambeth, London. It partook in several night patrols and was on the strength of No. 50 HDS RFC at Dover in February 1917. Built by Ruston Proctor & Co Ltd, of Lincoln, 2699 was six machines away from Robinson's 2693 on the production line.
2. Written notes, Ruth Leefe Irwin (née Robinson), March 1967.
3. Frederick Sowrey brought down Zeppelin *L32* over Billericay on the night of 24 September, 1916 – see Rimell, R. L.: *Zeppelin!* pp. 126-138.
4. Conversation: Mrs Vera Tate with author, 19 August, 1979.
5. Letter: W. L. R. to his sister Grace Leefe Robinson, April 1916.
6. Harold's 1914-15 Star, British War and Victory Medals, next-of-kin bronze plaque, various personal photographs and papers were auctioned together with his brother's VC at the November 1988 Christie's auction.
7. Neuman, G. P. (ed): *The German Air Force in the Great War*, p. 119.
8. Later Air Marshal Sir Arthur 'Bomber' Harris, who directed the RAF's air offensive over Germany in World War II as Commander-in-Chief, Bomber Command from 1942.
9. Harris's report, 26 April, 1916, PRO Air 1, 578/16/15/168, Part 1.
10. W. L. R.'s report, 26 April, 1916. PRO Air 1, 578/16/15/168, Part 1.
11. Major T. C. R. Higgins' report, 26 April, 1916. PRO Air 1, 578/16/15/168, Part 1.
12. Poolman, K.: *Zeppelins Over England*, p. 158.

Chapter Six

1. Rawlinson, A.: *The Defence of London 1915-1918*, p. 98.
2. *Ibid*, p. 104.
3. W. L. R.'s report, 2/3 September, 1916 – see *Appendix III*.
4. The sub-cloud car (*Spähkorb*) was developed by Ernst Lehmann and his executive officer in *ZX11*, *Freiherr* von Gemmingen, and was widely used by the Army Airship Division but generally shunned by the Navy. *LZ90*'s car is at the Imperial War Museum in Lambeth, London.
5. *Flight*, 7 September, 1916, pp. 761-2.
6. Letter: Harry Dobson to author, 9 March, 1976.
7. *Ibid*.
8. Letter: L. A. Aves to author, 14 September, 1976.
9. Letter: W. L. R. to his parents, 22 October, 1916 – see *Appendix VI*.
10. Letter: W. J. Clark to author, 31 May, 1976.
11. *L32* War Diary, PRO Air 1, 2585, p. 9.
12. Robinson, D. H.: *The Zeppelin in Combat*, p. 176.
13. In following weeks RFC airmen of No. 39 HDS accounted for naval Zeppelins *L32* and *L31*, while *L33*, crippled by gunfire, made a forced landing in

Little Wigborough, Essex, and its crew captured. For details of these and all other German airships brought down during the war, see *Zeppelin!*

14. Letter: L. A. Aves to author, 14 September, 1976.
15. Letter: W. L. R. to his parents, 22 October, 1916 – see *Appendix VI*.
16. Russell Mallinson, P.: 'Scareships!', *The London Magazine* (date unknown), p. 264.

Chapter Seven

1. Letter: A. J. Gogh to author, 15 July, 1976.
2. *The Daily Sketch*, 4 September, 1916, p. 2.
3. Walter, E. W.: *Heroic Airmen and their Exploits*, pp. 71-72.
4. Metropolitan Police Report, Sergeant F. Buttler of Y Division, Enfield, 4 September, 1916. PRO MEPO 2/1652.
5. For latest research into Schütte Lanz history, see Haaland, D.: *Der Luftschiffbau Schütte Lanz Mannheim Rheinau (1909-1925)*.
6. Robinson, D. H.: *The Zeppelin in Combat*, p. 36.

Chapter Eight

1. *The Daily Mail*, 6 September, 1916, p. 5.
2. Letter: Mrs D. Barclay to author, 12 August, 1978.
3. Metropolitan Police Report, Sergeant F. Buttler of Y Division, Enfield, 4 September, 1916. PRO MEPO 2/1652.
4. *Ibid*.
5. *Ibid*.
6. *Ibid*.
7. *Ibid*.
8. Arrangements made for burial of Zeppelin crew, Wednesday, 6 August [*sic*] 1916, Metropolitan Police report, Superintendent W. Crane of Y Division, Enfield, 5 September, 1916. PRO MEPO 2/1652.
9. The bogus reference to '*L21*' is perpetuated on Robinson's graveside epitaph and, until comparatively recently, on the memorial at Cuffley. It requires clarification. In July 1937 Douglas Robinson, the 'elder statesman of rigid airship history' visited the Air Ministry Library and discussed the question with J. C. Nerney, the then Chief Librarian: 'He called for all the original documents on the 2/3 September raid; here were track charts of the ships over England and messages from tracking stations, as well as radio intercepts. *L21* was clearly shown both reaching England and departing the coast. I am not sure if *SL11* was correctly identified by radio intercepts, though she surely was identified by examining the wreckage. (Army ships were identified by the first three letters of the CO's last name, so *SL11* should have been 'SCH'.) There was absolutely no doubt in the minds of either of us that *L21* was correctly identified, and we concluded that the '*L21*' number had been

pulled out of the air for no particular reason, as the public would have been severely disappointed if they had learned that the night's victim was *not* a Zeppelin.'

10. *The Barnet Press*, 16 September, 1916, p. 3.

11. *The Barnet Press*, 9 September, 1916, p. 5.

12. *The Barnet Press*, 16 September, 1916, p. 5.

13. *The Daily Graphic*, Monday, 4 September, 1916. The contravention of Section 35B could result in heavy penalties for souvenir hunters. Police and military forces spared no efforts in tracking down likely suspects; several men and women were taken before the courts and subsequently fined.

14. Holt's report, 5 September, 1916. PRO, FO 371, 12069.

15. PRO, FO 371, 12069.

16. *Ibid.*

17. *The Daily Mail*, 9 September, 1916, pp. 2-3.

18. Letter: Florence Mabel David to W. L. R., September 1916.

19. Letter: Lieutenant G. H. Lewis to his father, 17 September, 1916. From Lewis, G. H.: *Wings over the Somme*. In another letter, dated 25 September, he recorded another aside referred to an RNAS pilot who 'must have been a very good fellow, and even in these days when half the fellows in the corps earn a VC every other day ...'

20. Perfect, C. T.: *Hornchurch in the Great War*, p. 126.

21. Russell Mallinson, P.: 'Scareships!', *The London Magazine* (date unknown), p. 266.

22. Perfect, *op. cit.*, p. 130.

23. Conversation: Mrs Vera Tate with author, 19 August, 1979. At least one ex-39 HDS fitter recalled visits by actresses to the Suttons Farm aerodrome.

24. *Ibid.*

25. Letter: Jimmy Grinling to Frederick Sowrey, 1916.

26. Gran, T.: 39 HDS history, PRO Air 1, 691/21/20/39, p. 23. Captain Tryggve Gran (a native Norwegian) served with the RFC and later the RAF, having already made a name for himself prior to the war. Gran had been a skiing expert to Captain Robert Scott's ill-fated 1912 Antarctic expedition and a member of the relief party which found the bodies of Scott and his companions. Flying a Blériot monoplane, Gran also made the first flight across the North Sea, on 30 July, 1914; he died in January 1980 aged 90.

27. Letter: W. L. R. to his parents, 5 June, 1917.

Chapter Nine

1. 48 Squadron Mobilization. PRO Air 1, 128/15/40/167.

2. *Ibid.*

3. *Ibid.*

4. *Ibid.*

5. Letter: Captain E. N. Griffith to author, 3 October, 1978.

6. Information via the late D. Whetton.

7. Pilot Officer A. N. Leckler, Repatriated or Escaped Prisoner of War report, 8 November, 1919. PRO Air 1, 1207/204/5/2619.
8. Festner was killed in action on 25 April, 1917.
9. Gran, T.: *Under British Flag*, p. 65.
10. Via AVM Sir Frederick B. Sowrey, KCB, CBE, AFC.

Chapter Ten
1. The next three lines of the letter were censored.
2. Letter: W. L. R. to his parents, 5 June, 1917.
3. Letter: W. L. R. to his parents, 21 July, 1917.
4. Second Lieutenants Arthur A. Baerlin and J. V. Wischer of No. 16 Squadron were brought down in BE2g A2745 on 28 April, 1917 as Kurt Wolff's 23rd victory.
5. Second Lieutenant H. E. Hervey of No. 60 Squadron, flying Nieuport 17 A311, was brought down by anti-aircraft fire on 8 April; MacIntosh, of No. 2 Squadron, force-landed on 26 May in Nieuport 17 B1685 following a one-sided duel with four Albatros fighters.
6. Hervey, H. E.: *Cage Birds*, pp. 26-7.
7. Robinson's fellow escaper was brought down on 28 April, 1917, in Sopwith 1½ Strutter A993, Reece's observer being Second Air Mechanic A. Moult. It must be recorded that Robinson's many escape attempts earned him a mention in despatches, – see *Appendix VIII*.
8. Hervey, *op. cit.* pp. 43-44.
9. See *Appendix VII*.
10. Hervey, *op. cit.* p. 77.
11. *Ibid.* p. 78.
12. Durnford, H. G.: *The Tunnellers of Holzminden*, p. 35.
13. Via Mrs. R. G. Libin.
14. Letter: Annie C. Rogers to W. L. R., 1918.
15. Later Sir William Stephenson, a key figure in British espionage during World War II; he was code-named 'Intrepid'.
16. The late actor Ronald Adam, quoted in a letter from P. G. Cooksley to author, 10 January, 1976.
17. Durnford, *op. cit.*
18. Gran, T.: *Under British Flag*, p. 168.
19. Letter: E. Hildesheim to author, 21 January, 1976.

Chapter Eleven
1. Eyewitnesses in Harrow Weald in 1977 remembered Robinson's 'bent back', as did relatives of his tailor Mr Crook of Wood Street near Hornchurch.
2. W. L. R.'s death certificate, certified by W. S. Darby, 31 December, 1918.

3. This was W. L. R.'s sister Katherine (Kitty), who had married Baron Heyking on 4 July, 1917. They had two daughters; Rosemary, who died young, and Regina Gisela, who would later become the custodian of her uncle's VC and related memorabilia.

4. *The Harrow Observer*, 3 January, 1919.

5. Gran, T.: *Under British Flag*, p. 168.

6. For first-hand accounts of the Niemeyers, see Durnford, H. G.: *The Tunnellers of Holzminden*.

7. In 1929 Joan Whipple became the second wife of Major General J. M. Brockbank of Salisbury, Wiltshire, the major having dissolved his marriage to Eirene Marguirete Robinson the previous year. Joan Uppleby Brockbank was cremated at Mylor, near Falmouth, Cornwall, on 10 December, 1968.

8. *The Harrow Observer*, op. cit.

9. Horace and Elizabeth's surviving son and three daughters lived long and busy lives. Irene married Lieutenant Colonel T. S. Ross of the Indian Medical Service and they had two children: Harold Robert born on 11 September, 1917, and Mary Rose on 30 July, 1923. 'Bobby' Ross is the family's other hero, although his exploits as a commando in World War II are not widely known.

On 11 September, 1944, Lieutenant Ross, with 21 other officers and men under the command of Colonel Ivan Lyon, set out in a submarine for Singapore harbour. The plan (code-named 'Operation Rimau') was to capture a Chinese junk and take it into Singapore harbour under cover of darkness, when frogmen would attach limpet mines to the enemy ships. A junk was duly captured, and its Malay crew were bundled aboard the submarine while the British and Australian commandos sailed off in the junk, but were intercepted by a Japanese patrol boat. The commandos scuttled the junk and made for islands in the Malay Archipelago.

Ross and Lyon, with some of their comrades, were hunted by the Japanese on the island where they had taken refuge. The two officers engaged in a last-ditch gun fight before they died on 16 October, 1944, but this diversion enabled some of their men to get away. Ten of the commandos were captured and held in a prison camp, where they were well treated until the Japanese court-martialled them because they had not been in uniform when captured. This technically put them on a par with spies. They were condemned to death and given what the Japanese considered an honourable execution – by Samurai sword. In 1984 a posthumous medal, The Australian Commando Association's Cross of Valour, was presented to Mrs Rose David in honour of her brother's sacrifice. Their mother Irene died in 1962.

Ruth bore John Irwin two children and lived to the age of 82, while Katherine passed away in November 1955, when she was in her 70th year.

Appendices
1. PRO MEPO 2 1652.
2. PRO FO 371 12069.
3. Imperial War Museum file, 'Pilots' reports relating to the destruction of Zeppelins,' also PRO FO 371 12069.
4. PRO Air 1 547.
5. Official records, *Marine Luftschiffer Kameradschaft*, Hamburg.
6. Letter: W. L. R. to his parents, 22 October, 1916.
7. Via Mrs R. G. Libin.

Footnote
The above notes are designed to aid the reader in locating contemporary records and serve as a guide towards further study of sources. For those consulting original documents it should be noted that both belligerents initiated Summer Time in 1916 *viz*:
1916: Summer Time began 21 May; ended 1 October.
1917: Summer Time began 8 April; ended 17 September.
1918: Summer Time began 24 March; ended 30 September.
During these periods Greenwich Mean Time was advanced by one hour; there was no 'Double Summer Time'. Times quoted throughout the text have not necessarily been converted from GMT to Central European Standard Time.

BIBLIOGRAPHY

Official Documents

Air Historical Branch records in Class AIR 1 held at the Public Records Office, Ruskin Avenue, Kew, Richmond, Surrey.

'Pilots' Reports Relating to Destruction of Zeppelins' and maps of air raids held by the Imperial War Museum, Lambeth, London.

Contemporary newspapers held by The British Library's Newspaper Library, Colindale Avenue, London.

Books

Bowyer, Chaz. *For Valour – The Air VCs*. London: William Kimber, 1978.

Bruce, J. M. *Warplanes of the First World War – Fighters* (3 volumes). London: McDonald & Co Ltd, 1968/1970.

Bushby, John R. *Air Defence of Great Britain*. London: Ian Allan, 1973.

Durnford, H. G. *The Tunnellers of Holzminden*. London: Cambridge University Press, 1920.

Gran, T. *'Under British Flag'*. Norway: Glydendalske Boghandel, 1919.

Haaland, Dorothy. *Der Luftschiffbau Schütte-Lanz Mannheim-Rheinau (1909-1925)*. West Germany: Mannheim University, 1987.

Hervey, H. E. *Cage Birds* London: Penguin Books, 1940.

James, Admiral Sir William. *The Code Breakers of Room 40*. New York: St Martins Press, 1956.

Jones, H. A. *The War in the Air*, Volumes II and III. London: Oxford University Press, 1928-31.

Morison, Frank. *War on Great Cities*. London: Faber and Faber, 1937.

Morris, Joseph. *The German Air Raids on Great Britain*. London: Sampson Low, Marston & Co Ltd, 1935.

Perfect, Charles Thomas. *Hornchurch During the Great War*. Colchester: Benham, 1920.

Poolman, Kenneth. *Zeppelins Over England*. London: Evans Brothers Ltd, 1960.

Purnell's History of the First World War (8 volumes). London: Phoebus Publishing Co, 1969.

Rawlinson, Sir Alfred. *The Defence of London, 1915-1918*. London: Andrew Melrose, 1923.

Richthofen, *Freiherr* Manfred von. *The Red Air Fighter*. London: The Aeroplane & General Publishing Co, 1918.

Rimell, Raymond Laurence. *Zeppelin!* London: Conway Maritime Press, 1982.

Robinson, Douglas Hill. *The Zeppelin in Combat*. Oxford: G. T. Foulis & Co Ltd, 1962.

Stacke, Captain H. Fitz M., MC. *The Worcester Regiment in The Great War*. Kidderminster: G. T. Cheshire & Sons Ltd, 1928.

Sutton, Squadron Leader H. T. *Raiders Approach!* Aldershot: Gale & Polden Ltd, 1956.

Walter, E. W. *Heroic Airmen and their Exploits*. London: Kelly, 1917.

Periodicals

Lloyd, T. A. (Icarus) 'No. 39 Squadron'. *The Army, Navy and Airforce Gazette*, Volume LXIX. 1928.

Lloyd, T. A. (Icarus) 'Reminiscences of No. 39 HD Squadron, RAF'. *Air* August-December, 1929.

Lloyd, T. A. (Icarus) 'Memorial to No. 39 (HD) Squadron'. *Flight*, Volume XXIV, 1932.

Lloyd, T. A. (Icarus) 'The Zepp Strafers', *Popular Flying*, Volume II, No. 8, 1933.

Robinson, Douglas Hill with P. Amesbury. 'Hauptmann Wilhelm Schramm'. *Cross & Cockade Journal (USA)* Volume 13, No. 1, Spring 1972.

Other

The personal letters, records and papers of the late Captain William Leefe Robinson, VC, kept in trust by the family until 22 November, 1988, when, together with the Victoria Cross, other medals, related photographs and memorabilia they were auctioned to set up 'A Medal For Life'.